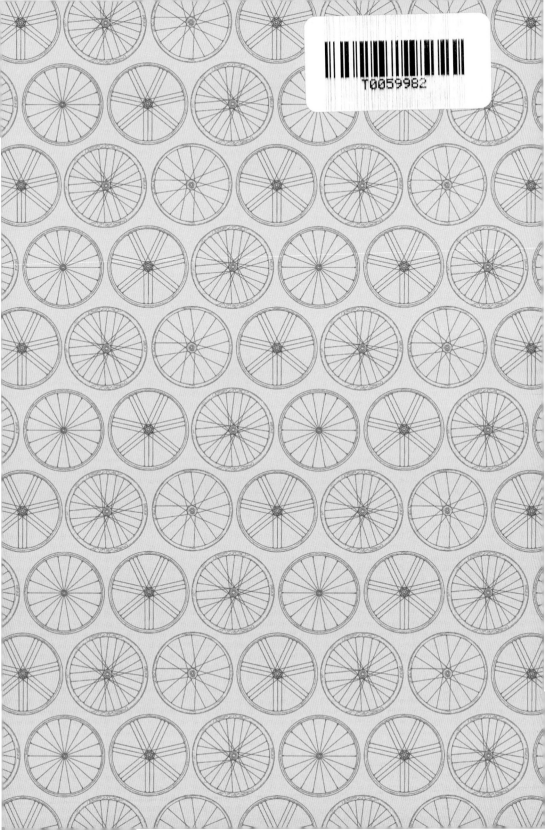

HOW TO
BUILD A BIKE
(IN A WEEKEND)

Published by
Laurence King Publishing Ltd
361–373 City Road
London EC1V 1LR
Tel: +44 (0)20 7841 6900
Email: enquiries@laurenceking.com
www.laurenceking.com

A catalogue record for this book is available from
the British Library.

ISBN: 978-1-78627-894-4

Commissioning editor: Zara Larcombe
Design: Alexandre Coco
Copyeditor: Nicola Hodgson

Printed in China

Laurence King Publishing is committed
to ethical and sustainable production.
We are proud participants in
The Book Chain Project®.
bookchainproject.com

*For my father, who encouraged me
to change my first derailleur.*

HOW TO
BUILD A BIKE
(IN A WEEKEND)

ALAN ANDERSON

Illustrations by Lee John Phillips

Laurence King Publishing

1

Planning, Budgeting & Buying 13

2

The Build Day One 47

3

The Build
Day Two

4

Maintenance

Build a bike!

Why build a bike? There's only one reason to have a bike — to ride it — and the best reason to build your own is that you get a better ride that way.

With complete control over the shape, size, weight and specification of the build, you can make the bike that perfectly fits you, and suits where, how and how often you ride. You can build one that can be loaded up with luggage, shopping or children, immediately making your daily routine easier. You can build one that is minimal and lightweight, for sport and speed, or one with sympathetic gearing and chunky tyres for going off-road or winching yourself up hills.

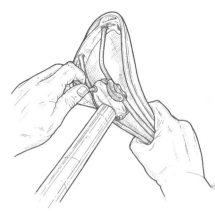

Cost is another factor. If you are making a bike for the long term, with good-quality components and a well-chosen frame, you'll find that assembling it yourself gives you much better value for money. You will need to invest a little, but the end result will be worth more than the sum of its parts.

Understanding how your bike is made, and how it works, will make you a better owner. You'll recognize the faint rattles, grinds and buzzes that are a bike's gentle first request for a little love, and know when to apply a drop of lubricant, twist a barrel adjuster, or tighten a spoke, each time preventing a trivial issue from turning into a serious one. Becoming a 'bike whisperer' like this has tangible benefits: it keeps you rolling along smoothly, gives the components a longer life, reduces repairs, and saves you the expense of professional servicing.

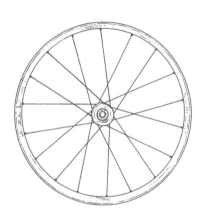

I love any bike shop, particularly an independent local one where the owner is a

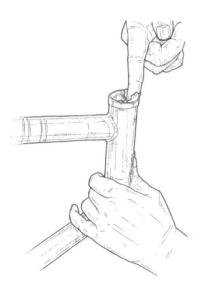

mechanic themselves, but you usually have to book services inconveniently far in advance, and pay a lot for jobs that you can easily do at home. If, however, you fit a component in the first place, you are well placed to fix it.

You'll be a better rider, too, with an instinctive feel for the bike's balance, manoeuvrability, weight, acceleration, braking and grip – and this translates into safer, quicker, more comfortable travel.

Over time, you'll develop a uniquely congenial relationship with the bike that you made, ride and maintain yourself. Like you, it will be unique, a one-off, with its own character and quirks; it is small wonder that many who build their own bikes also give them names.

Finally, when you enjoy riding, you ride more, and this is the most compelling reason to build your own bike. Every mile in the saddle does you good, making your body fitter and your mind calmer, and, while riding, you leave no waste in the air or on the ground. There's nothing like it.

So if, with a little planning, you can make one bike that will not only be a better ride, but also last longer, cost less, make you happier, and make the world a slightly better place, surely the right question to ask is not 'Why build a bike?', but 'Where do I start?'

About this book

With this book you'll gain the confidence to build your own bike, ending up with a machine that suits you perfectly and is ready to go wherever you want to take it. Having built the bike yourself, you'll understand how all the parts work together, and find it easy to tune, troubleshoot and keep in good condition.

This book is not a complete bike-building manual. The infinite variety of parts manufactured, and the easy availability of second-hand components, makes it impossible to cover every conceivable build: it would be literally thousands of pages long, and be out of date in a matter of weeks. That said, while parts that do the same job vary in the details, they tend to work on the same principles and are fitted in the same places on the bike. This book will show you how components work, what to consider when you are selecting them, and how to fit them. It will help you choose between rim or disc brakes, clincher or tubeless tyres, quill or threadless stems, for instance, and flat or drop handlebars.

Bike building is very educational, in a fun way. Most components these days are well designed, well made and a pleasure to work with, especially if you take the time to puzzle out how they actually work.

When fitting a new component, you should always refer to the manufacturers' instructions, but this book will guide you through the process so that you choose the right parts in the first place, and enjoy the build.

If you buy a complete bike from a store, you will ride it, but you won't ever love it in the same way as you love the bike that you have built yourself.

Sourcing components

The internet has become an amazing resource for bike builders, and it's inevitable that you will spend some happy hours double-checking minutiae like seat-tube diameter, bottom bracket type and crank arm length as you assemble the raw materials for your build. Get into the flow of it, don't be afraid to ask vendors questions and double-check everything. You will soon have a stack of components waiting for your attention: the raw materials for turning your dream machine into a reality. At the back of this book are checklists where you can note all of the necessary dimensions as you spec up your machine.

Anatomy of a bike

1 - Shifter (integrated brake and gear)

2 - Handlebar

3 - Cables (brake and gear)

4 - Tyre

5 - Rim

6 - Spokes

7 - Hub

8 - Brake disc

9 - Brake calliper

10 - Pedal

11 - Crankset

12 - Chain

13 - Rear derailleur

14 - Cassette

15 - Front derailleur

16 - Seatpost collar

17 - Seatpost

18 - Saddle

19 - Stem

20 - Steerer tube (with spacers)

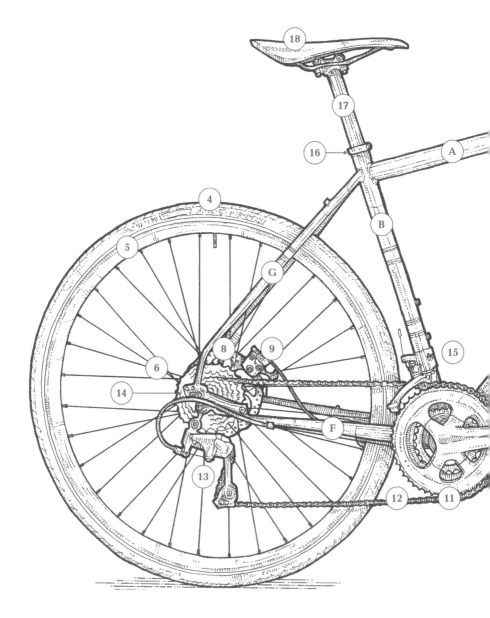

Frame

A - Top tube
B - Seat tube
C - Down tube
D - Head tube
E - Fork
F - Chain stay
G - Seat stay

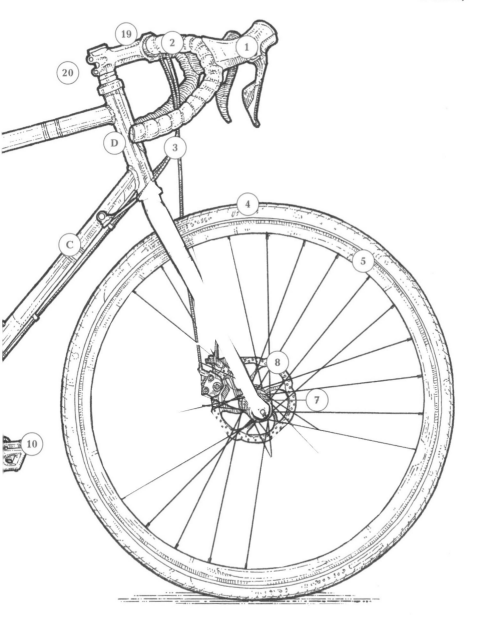

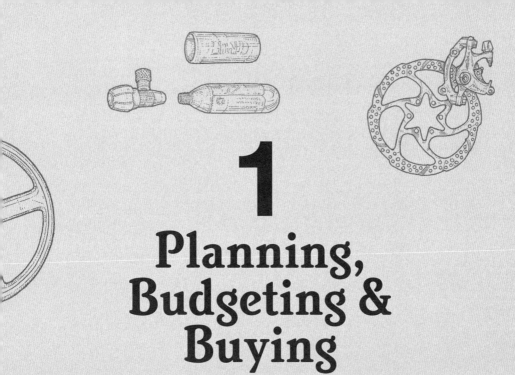

1

Planning, Budgeting & Buying

Assuming that you are building a bike from scratch, and not restoring and rebuilding one that you already have (an excellent activity in its own right), then careful preparation is crucial. This is the stage when you turn a daydream into a plan. As you select the parts, use the checklists on pages 123 and 124 to make sure that you don't forget anything, and that your selections will work together.

1.1 New and old

If, like me, you love cycling for its eco-friendly, affordable efficiency, then you will no doubt be interested in minimizing the cost and environmental impact of your build.

The good news is that you can do this without compromising significantly on quality: most well-made bicycle components (including shifters, brakes and derailleurs), if looked after, will last for decades – or thousands of kilometres of riding. Every bike I've built has been a mixture of old and new parts, and going second-hand is an excellent way to recycle and save money.

Components that you should probably buy new

These are the parts that experience the most friction, and will inevitably deteriorate with use; so, although second-hand examples may have plenty of life left in them, you're safer with new. Note that aluminium (alloy) wheels and frames can suffer from metal fatigue, which is invisible until they give way, so buying new is recommended unless you can be certain that they have only seen light use.

- Headset bearings
- Bottom bracket
- Chain and cassette
- Brake pads
- Wheels
- Tyres
- Cables
- Aluminium frames

Components that you can buy second-hand or recycle off an old bike

Literally everything not listed above – as long as it's been looked after.

Clean and grease everything before you reuse it, check for cracks, scratches, dings and bends, and you should be good to go.

1.2 Restoring a bike

Restoring an old, more or less complete bike is a great thing to do: it's probably cheaper than building your own from scratch, and you'll spend less time planning and more on the enjoyable business of bicycle mechanics.

You can either honour the machine's history, using second-hand vintage components to replace worn-out parts, or create something new, fitting modern brakes, gears and wheels to a classic frame. Either way, you'll end up with a unique bike with a ton of character.

That said, it is a less predictable business than building from scratch, and the older the frame is, the more likely you are to run into compatibility issues requiring online research, unusual tools, or help from your local bike workshop. While the main techniques of bike building are covered herein, issues of compatibility, vintage parts and the obsolete components of cycling's history are beyond the scope of this book. The resources on page 125 will help.

1.3 What kind of bike do you want?

One bicycle can serve as commuter, intercity tourer, shopper, on- and off-roader, and child transporter — and this versatility is part of the joy of owning and riding it.

It is surprisingly gratifying to break up a Saturday morning road circuit with a few kilometres along dirt tracks, towpaths or bridleways, and then use the same bike, panniers stuffed, to bring the weekly supermarket shop home. If you have a machine that can whip you through a 60km/h descent on a clear country road, and feel equally steady with a child on a carrier or tow-along, your life becomes simpler and richer: apart from the go-anywhere, do-anything sense of freedom it brings, it's just brilliantly convenient.

So, although you could use this book to build a stripped-down featherlight racer, or a rock-solid urban cargo carrier, I would suggest that, with a bit of care, you should be able to spec out and build a bike that is at once sporty and practical, strong yet not overly heavy.

That said, there's more than one way to skin a cat: this book does offer a few ways to solve the 'just one bike' puzzle, and you have to make some significant choices early on.

This bike will be equally good for commuting or recreational riding...

Do you want to make a bike that is, roughly speaking, a road model, with rim brakes, fairly narrow wheels and tyres and drop handlebars? This will bias you towards quicker on-road riding (although you will still be able to go off-road) and will make tours and sportives easier and faster.

Or do you want to use a gravel bike as your jumping-off point? This borrows some technology from mountain biking, with disc brakes, fatter tyres and, possibly, flat handlebars. It would be happier off-road, and robust for pot-holed city streets, but slower if you wanted to chew through a long circuit on a summer Saturday.

The two bikes that most of the illustrations are based on are examples of two contrasting approaches. One is a tough road bike that has also proven itself off-road on long trips, and on thousands of short hops around town carrying heavy loads, children and plenty of shopping. The other is a 'monstercross' or gravel model with many of the features of a mountain bike; this is just as useful as its sibling, but more sure-footed in the dirt, and with lower gearing that helps it deal with nasty climbs at the expense of super-fast descents. Both are steel, for strength, comfort, value and longevity. Whichever route you choose to go down, this book will help you decide what is important to you, and then advise you how best to design your bike so you end up with a machine that makes you happy.

...this one won't, although you'd need something like it for a speed-record attempt.

1.4 Choosing a frame

Passionate cyclists know that the frame is more than just the skeleton of your bike: it is its very soul. No matter how many times you change worn-out wheels, sprockets, chains, saddles, brakes or bearings, a bicycle remains the same bicycle if it has the same frame: and it influences your ride more than any other part of the machine.

The frame determines our posture when riding, the feel of vibrations and bumps from the road surface, the way that power is transmitted from your muscles through to the wheels, how balanced you are, how exposed you are to wind resistance, and how much control you have, both on- and off-road. The choice of frame material also determines the lifespan of your bike: so it makes sense to choose your frame, and corresponding forks, with care. The four big considerations are: material, size, shape (or geometry) and component compatibility. All of these factors interact with each other to affect the nature of your finished bike.

Material

The frame material not only determines the comfort of your ride, it also dictates its weight and how efficiently the energy from your pedal strokes is transmitted through to the ground. It influences the bike's lifespan, and how much luggage (or what size of passenger) you can carry safely.

Size

The size of the frame affects how comfortable you will be. You will always be able to ride a bike that is slightly too big or too small, and adjustments to saddle, stem and handlebars will help, but long rides will be uncomfortable and frustrating if the frame isn't the right size for your height and the length of your legs.

Component compatibility

You should also pay close attention to the kind of components that you will be able to fit. For instance, disc or centre-pull v-brakes require bosses or anchor points built into the frame; a narrow frame and fork combination will limit how wide your tyres can be; and rear carriers or mudguards also need fixing points. If you know that you want to carry luggage, or go off-road, you need to bear this in mind when selecting a frame.

Colour

A brightly painted bicycle can be a thing of real beauty, but there's something to be said for a deliberately unobtrusive bike: thieves are much less likely to be drawn to it. If you leave your bike locked up in public a lot, an unobtrusive dark grey or black frame is a good idea. Especially after dark, sober bicycles fade into the background, and attract less attention from the criminal fraternity.

Shape

Frame geometry refers to the angles formed at the points where the tubes of the frame meet each other. While the differences in these angles from one bike to another can seem minor, they have a crucial effect on your position and therefore on your comfort and the qualities of the ride.

Making your own frame

One way to ensure that your bike is unique is to commission a frame, having it made to your exact measurements, preferred geometry and personal material specifications. Specialist frame builders (usually working in steel) will walk you through the whole process; in some workshops you can wield the blowtorch yourself to weld your own frame together. While this results in a uniquely personalized bike, it is expensive.

1.5 Frame material

Traditional bike-builder wisdom has it that some compromise is inevitable: 'light, strong or cheap: pick two' summarizes the necessary trade-off that is the first decision you need to make as you plan your build.

Despite experiments with plastic and bamboo, the vast majority of bike frames manufactured are made of one of only four materials: steel, aluminium, titanium or carbon fibre. Each has advantages and disadvantages.

Steel

This has the longest and most storied history: it has been used to make bikes for well over a century, and the great racers of cycling's heroic era all rode on steel frames.

From the point of view of the amateur bike-builder, it has many advantages. Its strength makes it the natural choice if you plan to carry a load, and its elasticity makes your ride comfortable, as the frame will absorb road buzz and vibrations. The same elasticity also means that steel doesn't suffer from metal fatigue, and it will last forever (as long as it's not allowed to rust). A steel bike is a bike for life. Finally, steel's long history and popularity mean that a high-quality frame is comparatively cheap, and good second-hand frames are easily available.

The downside is that steel frames weigh more than their titanium, aluminium or carbon-fibre equivalents.

> **TIP:** When choosing a steel frame, make sure that it is double-butted (reinforced internally with extra-thick tubes at points of stress) and made of a strong, light alloy. Reynolds tubes are well regarded and popular with British manufacturers in particular.

LUGS

A classic steel frame like this one has narrow tubes, elegantly sweeping forks, and lugs (socket-like sleeves) at the points where tubes meet.

Titanium

This wondrous metal has several properties that make it highly desirable: it's half the weight of steel, twice as strong as aluminium, immune to corrosion and comfortably elastic. The downside? Cost. Working with titanium is complicated, as it can't be welded in the presence of oxygen, and is much more expensive than manufacturing with steel or aluminium. This, in turn, means that new frames are expensive, and second-hand ones rare. If you can afford a titanium frame, consider it seriously, and look after it carefully. The unpainted finish that distinguishes many titanium bikes also makes them conspicuously visible to thieves.

Aluminium (often known as alloy)

Cheaper and lighter than steel, and easy to manufacture tubes from, this is the most popular material for bike frames at the budget end of the market. However, it is less popular with committed cyclists and bike builders for two reasons. First, aluminium frames are less elastic than steel, and therefore more rigid and uncomfortable. Second, aluminium (again unlike steel) is subject to metal fatigue in normal use. All aluminium frames will eventually start to crack and then fail: if you ride regularly, ride hard, carry luggage, ride off-road, or are heavy yourself, this process will be accelerated. Sadly, an aluminium bike will always be mortal.

Carbon fibre

The material of choice for lightweight racing bikes, carbon fibre is incredibly light and strong. Frames can be made rigid in some areas and flexible in others, giving both excellent transmission of power and a comfortable ride, but there is a downside. Carbon fibre is not good with local high pressures, making it susceptible to catastrophic failure in the event of a collision, or even the strain of an over-tightened bolt: one distinguished frame designer warns that over-zealous maintenance is a greater hazard than crashing. An accurate torque wrench is therefore essential to perform even the simplest jobs, but if you take care with that, and don't have any high-impact crashes, a good carbon frame will last a lifetime.

Carbon fibre is much more flexible from a design point of view, as bike designers aren't constrained by the necessity of working with tubes; many carbon frames have distinctive, innovative shapes.

A performance-oriented frame can take full advantage of carbon fibre's high strength-to-weight ratio.

1.6 Frame size and stem length

You might think that it would be easy to pick a frame that is the right size — after all, most are manufactured in only five — but look around, and you'll see plenty of your fellow cyclists either stretched out over frames that are too large, or hunched over ones that are too small. Evidently it's easy to get it wrong!

Even though you can tweak the exact fit with careful placement and adjustment of saddle, seatpost, handlebars and stem, the frame itself needs to be appropriately sized – if it isn't, you're looking at a lifetime of slightly frustrating riding.

A good place to start is by looking at the bike you currently ride. Do you find it comfortable, even after a few hours in the saddle? Does your back feel relaxed, neither stretched nor squashed? Does your weight feel well distributed between the front and back wheels? When you stand over the bike, is your groin clear of the top tube by a couple of centimetres or more? Is a good length (at least 10cm) of seatpost visible? Do your knees open fully as you pedal? If the answer to all these questions is 'yes', then your bike probably fits you pretty well – use its size as a starting point for your build.

Stems (short tubes that join the steerer tube to handlebars) also affect your comfort considerably. A longer stem will stretch your torso and arms out, a short one will compress them: it's a matter of personal preference as to which position you prefer. They vary in length from 50mm to about 140mm, with most people using something in the middle like 100–110mm. If you are tall, or have short legs for your height, consider a longer stem; if you are short, or have short legs for your height, go shorter. If you're uncertain, it's a sensible idea to buy a couple of different sizes to try out, choose the one that you prefer, and return the other.

What to measure

There are two reasons why you can't simply use your height and the stated size of a bike frame to confidently make a rapid decision. First, you need to take account of not only your overall height, but also the length of your legs. For instance, based on height alone I would fit a large frame, but my legs are long. This makes my torso short, so I find a medium bike is actually a better fit, with a high seatpost that allows my legs to extend fully. Other riders with short legs and longer torsos have the opposite issue. For that reason, you should refer to both columns in the chart opposite. If they give you the same result, then your decision is easy. If they differ, then favour the measurement that fits your torso: it's easy to move a saddle up and down so your legs are comfortable, but you can't stretch or contract a top tube that is the wrong length.

Sizing scales

The second consideration is that mountain-bike-type frames are sized in inches based on the distance between the centre of the bottom bracket and the top of the seat tube. Road bikes use the same distance, but in the metric system, so size is given in centimetres. Road or mountain, the obvious problem with this is that this distance is not only a function of the size of the whole frame but also the angle of the top tube. This can be nearly horizontal, or slope downwards dramatically, making significant variation possible.

1

Start with this chart
based on your height.

2

Now compare the results
with your inside leg.

| Height | Inside Leg | FRAME SIZE | |
		Road	Mountain
Up to 5'3"/160cm	29"/75cm	50cm	15"–16"
5'4"–5'6" 162–168cm	29½"/76cm	51cm	15"–16"
	30"/77cm	52cm	15"–16"
	30½"/78cm	52cm	16"–17"
5'7"–5'9" 170cm– 175cm	31"/79cm	53cm	16"–17"
	31½"/80cm	54cm	16"–17"
	32"/81cm	54cm	17"–18"
5'10–5'11" 177cm–180cm	32¼"/82cm	55cm	17"–18"
	32½"/83cm	56cm	18"–19"
	33"/84cm	56cm	18"–19"
	33½"/85cm	57cm	20"–21"
6'0–6'2" 182–188cm	34"/86cm	58cm	20"–21"
	34¼"/87cm	58cm	20"–21"
	34¾"/88cm	59cm	20"–21"
6'3"+/190cm+	35"/89cm	60cm	20"–21"
	35½"/90cm	62cm	22"+

Measuring your inside leg

Note that the full inside-leg measurement is
not the same as the inseam measurement
you use for fitting trousers. You won't get
an accurate result if you try to measure
this distance alone, and the label of your
jeans is definitely not reliable enough.
Stand in your socks on a flat surface with
your feet apart, then hold one end of a
measuring tape into the top of your leg at
the groin while a friend holds it taut to the
floor next to your heel and reads off the
measurement. Make a note of it.

Standing over a bike gives a quick idea of
its fit. You should have a gap of at least a
couple of centimetres between groin and
crossbar: this bike is too large for the rider.

1.7 Frame shape and geometry

Even though carbon-fibre bikes are made in a host of distinctive shapes, the basics of bike geometry have remained the same for many years, and you only need to look for a few angles to get a sense of how the bike will ride.

Bike manufacturers will have all of this information on their websites (along with a host of other measurements), but it can be hard to know how to interpret it. These are the essentials to bear in mind when reading reviews or comparing two frames' specifications:

1 - Wheelbase

This is the horizontal distance between the centres of the front and rear axles and affects how the bike handles: a longer wheelbase results in more comfort and stability, so most leisure bikes (including mountain bikes, tourers, hybrids and gravel bikes) tend to have a longer wheelbase. The bike's steering is also less responsive, making it less twitchy and easier to balance. A shorter wheelbase results in more efficient power transmission and more responsive steering, so racing bikes are built along these lines.

2 - Chainstay length

Related to the wheelbase, this is the distance from the centre of the bottom bracket to the centre of the rear axle. As with the wheelbase, a short chainstay results in a faster, but less stable, bike.

3 - Head tube angle

The angle of the head tube from the horizontal affects the bike's steering, stability and riding position. The steeper it is, the less effort is required to steer – and the less stable the bike is.

Tourers and mountain bikes generally have low head angles: the former because a stable ride is important; the latter because of the increased control that it provides when navigating uneven and rough terrain. Racing bikes have steep head angles; these not only allow for rapid manoeuvrability during a race, but also position the rider further forward for aggressive riding.

Head tube angles vary as follows (the differences seem small, but they make a surprising difference to the quality of the ride):

TYPE	HEAD TUBE ANGLE	STYLE
Pro racing bike	73° or higher	Aggressive
Tourer	72°	
Gravel bike	71°	
Hybrid/Urban bike	70° or lower	
Mountain	70° or lower	Relaxed

4 - Effective top tube

Traditionally, this tube was horizontal, or very nearly horizontal: these days, it is usual for it to slope downwards from the head tube to the seat tube, and the angle at which it does this can vary dramatically. For that reason, you shouldn't compare top tube lengths on different bikes: instead, use the effective (or 'virtual') top tube measurement. This is the length of an imaginary horizontal line between centre of the seat tube or seatpost, and the centre of the head tube. This measurement is crucial in choosing a bike that is the right size for you.

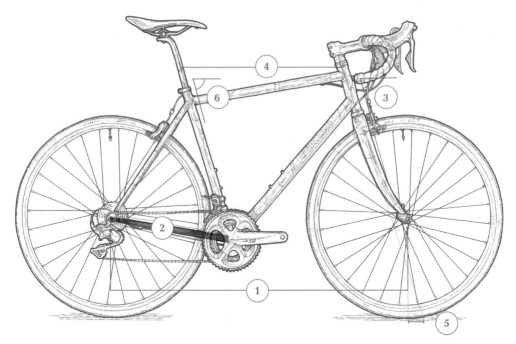

5 - Fork trail

This is another key factor in handling. To visualize it, imagine one straight line from the centre of the fork steerer tube all the way to the ground. The point where it hits the ground is the steering axis. Now imagine another line dropping perpendicularly from the centre of the wheel to the ground, touching it at the tyre patch. There will be a distance, known as the fork trail, between the steering axis and the tyre patch: on most bikes, this distance will be between about 50mm and 63mm. The longer it is, the more stable the bike will be: 57mm of trail is considered a sweet spot between responsivity (a short trail) and steadiness (a long trail).

6 - Seat tube angle

This determines how far behind the pedals you sit: the further back, the more relaxed you will be, but moving forwards, over the pedals, allows you to drive down more powerfully on them. The seat tube angle does not vary as much as the head tube angle, and is generally between 71 and 75 degrees, with a higher value being more race-oriented. This angle is not necessarily final, though: you can tinker with it by moving your saddle forwards or backwards.

Step-through frames

Designed for riders who wanted to wear a long skirt while riding, the step-through frame (with a much lower top tube) is also a practical solution if you want to be able to mount and dismount easily, and enjoy an upright position: it is therefore the shape of the classic 'Amsterdammer' urban bike. However, it is struturally weaker than a conventional frame, which means that the tubes need to compensate by being thicker; this makes it a heavier design.

1.8 Frame and brake compatibility

The choice of frame determines a few other important aspects of the bike's specification. Before you make the final decision, be sure that the frame you like will accept the brakes that you want.

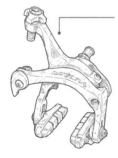

Rim brakes

Rim brakes (which usually use a calliper system to pinch on the wheel's rim with rubber pads) were the standard for many years, and are still fitted to many road and hybrid bikes. They are reliable and effective – except when it rains. Wheel rims and pads become slippery when wet (even if you take care to feather the brakes while riding, regularly brushing water off the surfaces), and there is nothing worse than not being able to stop, fast, in traffic, when you need to. Off-road, they present a different problem: mud can be carried up by the tyre and clog brake callipers completely. That said, for cycling on roads, rim brakes work just fine most of the time.

Disc brakes

When mountain biking took off, there was a need for brakes that were reliable in bad conditions yet powerful enough to cope with rapid off-road downhills. Solving this problem, the first disc brakes were launched in 1997. Disc brakes are effective when wet, and allow for lighter rims and wider tyres than calliper brakes; so, in due course, road bikes started to adopt them. Locating the brake at the centre of the wheel (rather than its rim) subjects the wheel, fork and frame to very different forces. You can't simply switch out old rim brakes and replace them with discs: manufacturers designate disc-compatible frames as such, so if a frame's name doesn't mention the braking, it will be rim-brake compatible. The same principle applies to wheels.

When inspecting a frame online or in person, you can immediately tell – a disc-compatible frame has bosses at the junction of the seat stay and chain stay, where the calliper units are fitted, whereas a rim brake set-up doesn't. A disc-compatible fork will have similar mounting points on the left side. You should also double check whether the frame uses a flat-mount or post-mount design to attach the brake callipers. Most new frames have flat mounts (holding the callipers flush to the frame and fork): some older ones have post mounts (holding the callipers proud of the frame and fork). Check when purchasing the frame which standard it uses, and make sure that your chosen brakes match: alternatively, adapters are available that allow you to fit post-mount brake units to flat-mount frames (but not vice versa). There is little difference in fitting and use. Another thing to bear in mind is that rotors are available in four sizes, 140mm, 160mm, 180mm or 200mm in diameter. The size that you need is determined by the position of the mounts on your frame, so check what your frame will take before purchase.

1.9 Pannier and mudguard mounts

When picking a frame, ensure that it will carry what you want it to, and check to see if it has carrier- and mudguard-mounting points.

Rack lug

If you are planning on touring, shopping or weekending on your bike, you will need a rear carrier; this, in turn, means that you'll need mounting points to attach it to. Check the frame to see if there are lugs at the base of the seat stays; pure racers don't have them, but touring bikes, gravel bikes and more versatile frames will. Usually, there are mounting points at the top of the seat stay, too. If there aren't, don't worry: a rack can still be fitted. A dedicated touring bike will also have mounting points on the front fork.

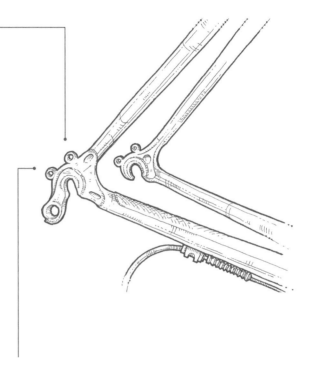

Mudguard lug

Mudguards, too, need lugs on the front fork and seat stays (panniers and mudguards can usually share a lug if you only have one on each side). Many riders, this author included, prefer to go without mudguards, finding them more weight and trouble than they are worth, but if you plan to go riding on wet roads in groups, or in office clothes that you want to keep clean, you should fit them.

1.10 Forks and shock absorbers

A good-quality frame and appropriately inflated tyres will give you a comfortable ride on most roads. Do you also need shock absorbers?

Mountain bikes with large shock absorbers on the front forks, and sometimes a suspension system on the rear wheel, are a common sight off-road and on it. If you plan to do a lot of riding, especially jumps, or fast or downhill riding, on rough trails and paths, this is the kind of model you should go for: so, build a mountain bike! For most of us, riding most of the time on the road, shock absorbers aren't a necessity.

The advantage of shock absorbers is that they allow the wheel to move in relation to the frame: and the further it can move (or 'travel'), the more impact it can absorb. The principal disadvantages are weight and cost: most shock-absorbing forks tip the scales at over 2 kilograms – making them two or three times the weight of steel or carbon forks, or the weight of an entire steel frame. Having many more parts, they are also more expensive, need more maintenance, and affect your handling and steering, particularly when braking and turning at speed, in a way that takes some getting used to. That said, they yield a much more comfortable ride over cobbles, and make kerbs easier to negotiate.

Smaller rear shock absorbers are increasingly common on high-end carbon road- and gravel-bike frames. Weighing less than front-mounted shocks, and with only a fraction of the travel, they dissipate the buzz and vibration of the road surface for a more comfortable ride.

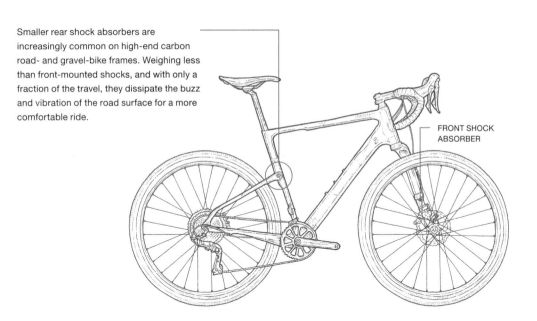

FRONT SHOCK
ABSORBER

A mountain bike like this has long-travel shock absorbers for both front and back wheels, which lets the bike soak up the energy of a heavy landing.

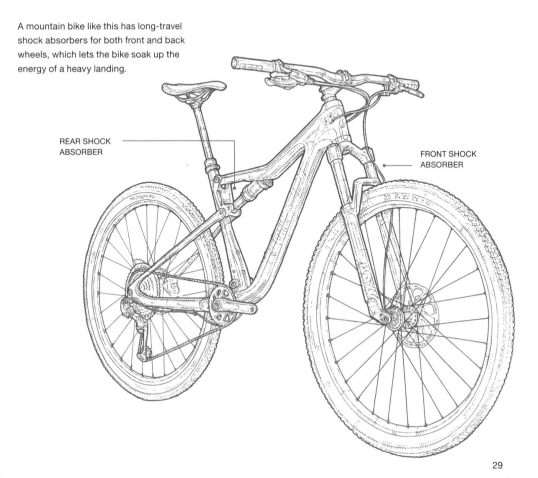

REAR SHOCK
ABSORBER

FRONT SHOCK
ABSORBER

1.11 Choosing handlebars

Handlebars are very simple components but they will make a massive difference to the quality of your ride, so you should give their shape and size some thought before you buy.

Broadly speaking, your choice is likely to be between flat (or nearly flat) bars and drops, but there are other patterns that lend themselves to particular specialisms. Nearly all bars are made of either aluminium or carbon fibre; there's not much difference in use or weight, but carbon fibre is usually more expensive.

Riser bars

These are wider than drops and will be more stable in rough situations, or if you are carrying a heavy load – which is why mountain bikes have them. They vary in width from about 740mm to 800mm, and the wider they get, the more stable (and, at the same time, harder to store indoors, or steer through gaps in traffic). Steering is precise, and fitting bar bags and carriers is easy. Fit flat-bar brake handles, shifters and grips. You only have one riding position, but it's comfortable.

Flat bars

Very similar in feel to risers but, being completely straight, have the wrists in a slightly less comfortable position. They vary in width from around 740mm to 800mm and also use flat-bar brake handles, shifters and grips.

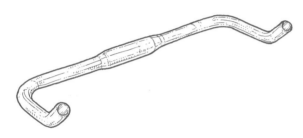

Bullhorns

Curving up and forwards, these look distinctive and, if you want to ride fast, can get you into an aerodynamic tuck very easily. Pick these if quick riding (and powerful climbing) are important, you want to set the bars some distance below your saddle, and you don't mind having a limited selection of riding positions. Use bar-end mounted brakes and gear shifters.

Drop bars

Perennially popular, drop bars offer great aerodynamics when you want to go fast (or are riding into the wind), a variety of riding positions, keeping you comfortable on a long ride, and a comparatively narrow profile – making them easy to store and squeeze through narrow gaps. They vary in width from around 380mm to 440mm: if you have broad shoulders, you may find a wider set more comfortable and more stable off-road. Fit drop-bar brake levers and gear shifters.

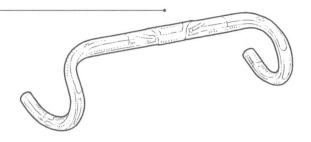

Flared drops

Opening out to give the rider more stability on the drops, these are popular on gravel bikes, which are more often ridden off-road. Fit drop-bar brake levers and gear shifters, but be careful how you position them as the bars' flare makes the shifters feel quite different in the hand.

Aero bars

Great for aerodynamics; poor for climbing; terrible for riding through traffic. These are strictly for racing and, even then, not for racing in groups.

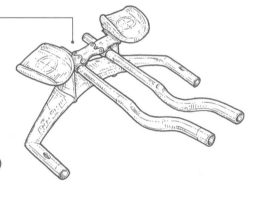

Butterfly bars

Very ungainly looking, butterfly bars come into their own when you're touring. There is plenty of space for lights, bags, phone mounts, bottle cages and the like; and they offer many different positions, making your shoulders, wrists and back more comfortable. Most often, flat-bar shifters and brake handles are fitted.

TIP: When you have decided on the shape and length of your bars, check their tube diameter and make sure that the stem is compatible.

1.12 Wheels

After the frame, the wheels are the most important parts of the bike: nothing else makes such a difference to how easy, quick and comfortable your ride is.

The complete bikes that you see in-store are often let down by the quality of their wheelsets, and one of the major advantages of building your own bike is that you can ride on lighter, stronger, faster-rolling wheels than you otherwise would. As always with cycling components, it is possible to spend a fortune on featherlight high-end gear, but also possible to get something that is extremely good without breaking the bank.

As wheels are subject to wear and tear, you should buy them new. At the high end, wheel rims can be made of carbon fibre, which is light and strong, but for most riders, a good alloy rim represents better value for money. Steel rims are heavy but robust – worth considering if you need a bike to be truly bombproof and aren't worried about speed, or hills.

Most new wheels are sold with freehubs, spare spokes and (if appropriate) disc brake fittings included. The basic considerations to bear in mind are as follows.

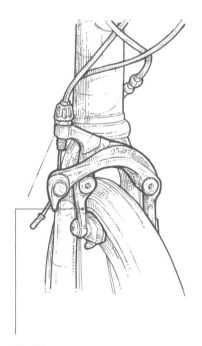

Braking
Rim brakes and disc brakes make different demands of the wheels, which are, accordingly, built differently depending on the braking system. A wheel is therefore either disc- or rim-brake compatible – it can't be both.

Freehubs and freewheels

Most rear wheels are supplied with a freehub onto which the sprockets of the rear cassette are slotted and fixed in place by a lockring. This is a considerable improvement on the freewheel system, standard for many years, which has a thread on the hub onto which a cassette is screwed. The freehub-plus-cassette system is easier to remove and maintain, offers greater flexibility, and is standard with today's groupsets.

Freehub compatibility

New wheels are usually supplied with a freehub that will be compatible with 8-, 9- or 10-speed cassettes: if you intend to fit an 11-speed cassette, you must get an 11-speed freehub. A major compatibility issue is that Campagnolo freehubs only accept Campagnolo's cassettes. SRAM and Shimano cassettes and freehubs are mutually compatible, but you should take care when ordering that you specify the correct freehub for the groupset you intend to use. In general, choosing a Shimano system will make the bike more convenient to build, maintain and repair, as more bike shops keep Shimano components in stock (see page 35 for more information on these manufacturers).

Diameter

There are two naming conventions for wheel size: mountain bike wheels are identified by their approximate diameter (when tyres are fitted) in inches; road, or cyclocross, wheels by their approximate diameter (when tyres are fitted) in millimetres.

The vast majority of road, touring, gravel and cyclocross bikes are fitted with 700C wheels, and your choice of wheel is widest in that size. If you are building with a road-geometry frame but off-road riding is going to be important to you, you should consider a 650C wheelset as a possible alternative, as it will usually allow you to fit chunkier, fatter tyres. Many gravel bikes come fitted with 650C wheels.

NAME	DESCRIPTION	WIDTH	STANDARD
700C	Fitted on nearly all road and cyclocross bikes, and identical in diameter to a 29" mountain-bike wheel.	Up to 45mm	ISO 622
650B	Slightly smaller alternative for gravel bikes, which allows fatter tyres to be fitted. Identical in diameter to a 27½" mountain-bike wheel.	Up to 50mm	ISO 584
29"	Also known as '29er', the largest wheels for mountain bikes: commonly used for cross-country rather than jumping or downhill riding.	50mm+	ISO 622
27½"	A mid-sized mountain-bike wheel identical in diameter to a 650B.	50mm+	ISO 584
26"	Traditionally the most popular size for mountain bikes, and too small for road or cyclocross frames. The smaller diameter is lighter and offers quicker acceleration and better agility at the cost of stability.	50mm+	ISO 559

Spoke count

All other things being equal, a wheel with more spokes will be stronger but heavier than one with fewer spokes. However, the quality of the build makes a significant difference too. Spoke patterns vary and depend on the braking system.

Front wheels with rim brakes can have a radial spoke pattern (in which the spokes run straight out from the hub to the rim without crossing each other) with as few as 18 spokes but great strength for their weight. Rear wheels and wheels with disc brakes must have spokes that cross over each other in a laced pattern: this allows them to cope with the torque generated between the braking or pedalling forces at the hub, and the rim. The more times a spoke crosses another spoke in the lacing pattern, the stronger the wheel will be.

For most riders, between 28 and 36 spokes should be strong enough: sometimes, rear wheels have more spokes than front wheels to compensate for the additional load and stress they bear.

A lightweight racing rear wheel with 21 spokes in a 2-cross lacing pattern

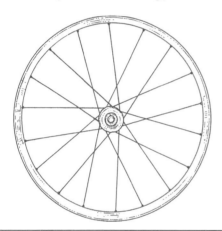

A distinctive 21-spoke rear wheel

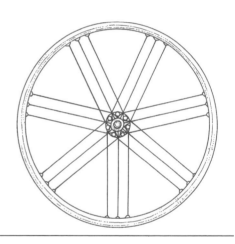

A 28-spoke rear wheel with a 4-cross lacing pattern

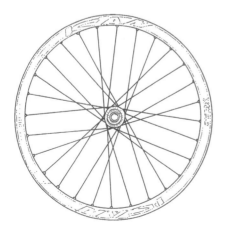

A lightweight 18-spoke radially spoked front wheel (for rim brakes only)

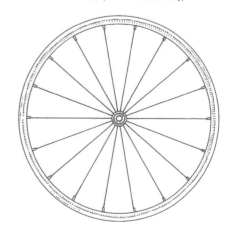

Rim width

Another factor that will be influenced by where you want to ride, and your choice of tyres, is the width of the rim. Whether you're rolling on clincher or tubeless, the fit between rim and the tyre bead has to be very tight, so narrow rims demand narrower tyres, and wide rims, wider tyres. Most pure 'road' rims will accept a tyre that's 23–28mm wide, and should go as wide as 32mm. To go wider than that – recommended if you want to go off-road – start looking at narrow 29er rims, or dedicated cyclocross or gravel-bike rims.

Tyres: clincher or tubeless?

For many years, clincher tyres (with a separate inner tube and outer tyre) were the norm, but tubeless tyres (with just the outer tyre) have become very popular. Make sure that the wheelset you choose is compatible with the tyres that you want to use on them.

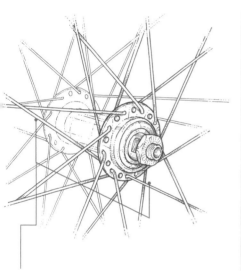

Axle width/spacing

The axle needs to be the same width as the space between the dropouts (a fork that allows the rear wheel to be removed without derailing the chain) on the frame and fork. Nearly all new front forks have a standard internal width (or spacing) of 100mm: rear axles are wider, with 130mm the standard for road bikes with rim brake fittings, and 135mm for disc brake systems. Older frames and forks may vary from these dimensions, so if you are undertaking a restoration job, you should measure the spacing (between the inside surfaces of the dropouts) by hand before ordering wheels.

Campagnolo vs Shimano vs SRAM

It's a near-certainty that your bike will have components from at least one of these manufacturers: between them, they dominate the market in bike gear (although they don't make frames or tyres). It's worth considering each make in turn before taking the plunge and choosing which to go for. All of them produce components at a wide range of price points, with their leading groupsets (see page 36) similarly priced.

Campagnolo are the aristocracy: an Italian company with a storied history, who fitted out many of the racing bikes of cycling's golden age. Focussing on road-bike parts (it took them many years to release a disc brake), they make components that are elegant and high performance, but sometimes a little idiosyncratic. Parts may also require specific Campagnolo tools, which can themselves be expensive, for fitting or removal.

Shimano are the global giants. With a huge range that includes many cheaper components for cyclists on a budget, they are stocked in every bike store and their parts are noted for their reliability. While their designs are more functional and less elegant than Campagnolo's, the variety of their offering means that nearly every bike has some Shimano on it, somewhere.

SRAM are the upstart newcomers, coming from a mountain bike background, and making components that are often very innovative. Their patented 'double-tap' gear-change system, for instance, allows the rider to shift up and down gears with only one lever. Many of their parts are compatible with Shimano systems, making them simpler to build with – but, like Campagnolo, they don't come cheap.

1.13 What's in a groupset?

While the frame determines the feel of your ride, it's the mechanical parts that actually speed you up and slow you down. Taken together, the brakes, chain, crankset, derailleurs, cassette and shifters are known as the groupset.

The three largest manufacturers of groupsets are Campagnolo, Shimano and SRAM: all offer a range of groupsets ranging from quite expensive to eye-wateringly expensive. The higher ends of their ranges are aimed at people who race, and take minute weight savings very seriously. Most of us are more concerned with reliability and value for money.

Fortunately, the entry-level groupsets from all three manufacturers are excellent: there is little to choose between them for quality, weight or price.

Buying a complete new groupset is an easy way to guarantee that all of the parts you need are compatible, but it is possible to assemble one second-hand or from parts without sacrificing the quality of your ride. The only parts of the groupset that inevitably wear out are the chain, chainring (on the crankset) and rear sprockets (or cassette); if the other parts are kept clean, dry and appropriately lubricated, they should last for decades.

1 - Derailleur or mech?

Like many of racing cycling's key terms, 'derailleur' is French in origin. Literally meaning 'de-railer', it was first coined as long ago as 1889, and is universally understood. Some English speakers find it a mouthful, though, and use the simpler 'mech' as an alternative. Both terms are in wide use – so when searching for a front or rear derailleur online, remember to try 'mech' as a keyword, too.

The first compatibility issue will be between the shifters and rear derailleur: the indexing needs to match, so one click on the shifter translates into a movement up or down one gear. The range of gears (between 8 and 12 on the rear mech) also needs to be the same. You also need to make sure that your chain is appropriate for the number of sprockets on your rear cassette.

By and large, brakes, cranksets and front derailleurs are cross-compatible, even if the major manufacturers would prefer you not to think so, while some of the best disc brakes out there come from other manufacturers. One of the bikes featured in this book has a hodgepodge of second-hand Campagnolo and Shimano parts that works well together; the other, a SRAM groupset paired with TRP Spyre brakes, is equally reliable.

SHIFTERS

2 - Cogs or sprockets?

You may hear the chainring and the cassette referred to as 'cogs'. This is an inaccurate usage: cogs are circular gears that engage with other cogs – like the moving parts in a watch mechanism. The correct term for a ring that's engaged with a chain is a sprocket. The terms 'chainset' and 'crankset' are often used interchangeably.

3 - Crank length

Cranks vary in length from 160mm up to about 185mm (measured from the centre of the bottom bracket spindle to the centre of the pedal axle), although the majority are in the range of 160mm to 180mm. It is common for 175mm cranks to come fitted to larger bikes and 165mm or 170mm to smaller models. There is good evidence that, within that range, longer and shorter cranks are about as efficient as each other for power transfer; however, a shorter crank arm asks less of your joints, so if you aren't particularly flexible, that may be the better choice.

High-end electronic groupsets

The most expensive groupsets from all of the major manufacturers feature electronic shifting, which move your derailleurs at the push of a button rather than the press of a lever. Changes are quicker and more precise, you can customize the controls to suit your style, and you can mount multiple sets of controllers, letting you change gear easily, whatever position you are riding in. Undoubtedly, these are the kinds of performance benefits that competitive riders find irresistible. Equally undoubtedly, they come at a serious cost: value for money is not part of the equation. For that reason, and due to their vulnerability to theft, electronic groupsets are not covered in this book.

1.14 Choosing cassette and crankset

The sprockets on cranksets and cassettes come with varying numbers of teeth that have a major effect on how you will ride the bike, and you should carefully consider how you plan to ride your new bike before committing.

Most bikes use multiple sprockets on the crankset, with a front derailleur, to offer a wider range of possible gears. When choosing a cassette and crankset combination, first make sure that the number of sprockets on each is compatible with your rear derailleur and shifting system. Then think about the kind of riding you want to do...

A wide range for challenging rides

Will you be climbing hills, carrying heavy loads, or going for long rides in bad weather? If so, you should choose a rear cassette with a wide range, and one or two low gears (bigger sprockets) that will give you a useful spread of gear ratios for all circumstances. Choose a cassette with 11 or 12 teeth on the smallest sprocket, and 29 or more teeth on the largest (so, for instance, an 11–32 cassette, or a 12-29).

A 1x groupset showing the single chainring and a rear cassette with a wide range, including a large 50-tooth sprocket that gives you a very low gear for steep climbs.

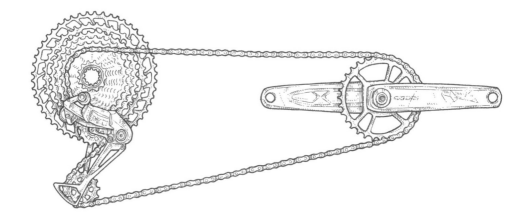

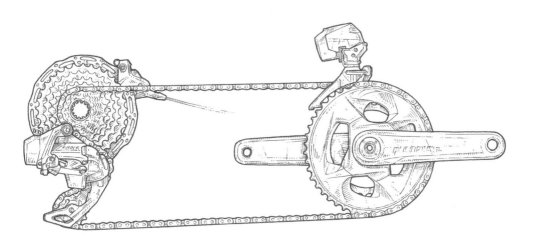

A high-end 2x road-racing groupset showing two chainrings on the crankset, and a rear cassette with a narrow range.

A narrow range for fast rides

 If you'll be riding on the flat, without loads, or are more interested in speed and performance, then a cassette with a tight range of high gears (smaller sprockets) will give you a bike that's easier to ride fast, matching a high gear to your preferred cadence. If you want a narrow range of higher gears, choose a cassette with 11 teeth on the smallest sprocket and 25 to 29 teeth on the largest (for instance, an 11–25, or an 11–27).

Cassette and derailleur compatibility

The rear derailleur has to be compatible with the cassette you choose: a wider range of gears demands a mech with a longer cage, so they come in three sizes: short, medium and long. When you choose the rear derailleur, make sure that it is compatible with the cassette that you have.

1.15 The chain

You need a new chain whether restoring an old bike or building a new one: it wears out faster than any other part and, unless you are absolutely sure that the chain is clean, will fit and has only been lightly used, it is not worth getting a second-hand one.

Which chain?

First, you need to make sure that it will work with the gearing you have chosen. The key factor is the number of sprockets (or speeds) in your cassette or freewheel.

SPROCKETS	MAKE	CHAIN
6/7/8 (or less)	Any	Any 6/7/8-speed chain
9	Shimano or SRAM	Any Shimano or SRAM 9-speed chain
10	Campagnolo	Campagnolo, KMC, Wippermann 10-speed chain
10	Shimano or SRAM	Shimano, SRAM, KMC, Wippermann 10-speed chain
11	Campagnolo	Campagnolo, KMC, Wippermann 11-speed chain
11	Shimano or SRAM	Shimano, SRAM, KMC, Wippermann 11-speed chain

Chain length

The other factor is chain length. Most chains are sold as 114 or 116 links, which is enough for most bikes (you'll probably need to remove links). However, if you are building with a large or extra-large frame, a long-cage derailleur and large sprockets, you may find that the full chain isn't long enough – this applies to SRAM 1x systems on large bikes in particular. If that is the case, buy two identical chains so that you can graft some links from one onto the other. Keep the spare chain safe and clean so you can repeat the process next time.

Make sure there is a 'power link' that enables the chain to be fitted easily by hand. Power links are outer links and have to connect two inner links. Different manufacturers have different trade names for these, including 'missing link', 'power lock' and 'connex', but they all look similar and work in the same way.

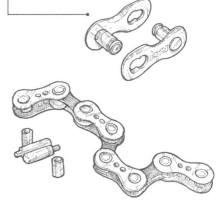

Campagnolo's Ultra-Link is different from other power links: it requires an expensive special tool, without which the link is easily broken. So, if you're building on a budget, avoid it.

1.16 Seatpost and saddle

Nothing will destroy your enjoyment of your bike like an uncomfortable saddle at the wrong height.

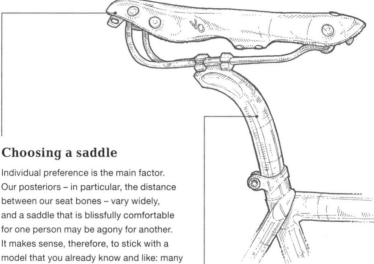

Choosing a saddle

Individual preference is the main factor. Our posteriors – in particular, the distance between our seat bones – vary widely, and a saddle that is blissfully comfortable for one person may be agony for another. It makes sense, therefore, to stick with a model that you already know and like: many riders move the same saddle from old bike to new more than once.

As a rule of thumb, if your riding position is aggressive (if your bars are significantly lower than your saddle, for instance, or you spend long periods on the drops), you should go for a flat, narrow saddle with less padding for the seat bones. Conversely, if you like a more upright position, get a wider saddle with more support at the back. Another indicator is your own flexibility: if, when standing, you can touch your toes easily, a flat saddle is more likely to suit you.

If you experience discomfort, pain or symptoms of poor circulation (numbness or pins and needles), then consider saddles with vents down the centre: they look unusual, but reduce pressure on the genitals of female riders and prostates of male riders, and allow blood to circulate more freely, reducing numbness and improving comfort.

Choosing a seatpost

The vast majority of seatposts are circular tubes of aluminium or carbon fibre. Some have shock-absorbing designs or mechanisms, but will still fit in the same way to the frame. Always double-check that the seatpost is compatible with the seat tube when you buy one, as they come in many diameters. Some carbon bikes with aero designs have oval cross-sections, in which case the post will be specific to that model and won't fit other bikes.

1.17 Pedals

Standard equipment for a century, toe-clips have now been superseded by clipless systems, in which a cleat on your shoe clips directly onto the pedal. Your choice is between that or a flat pedal, on which your foot rests and is not attached.

Clipless pedals

You'd be right to point out that a device that clips your shoe to the pedal is not at all 'clipless', but for better or worse, that is how they are known. Cleats screwed onto the sole of the shoe lock into a mechanism on the pedal, holding the foot firm, keeping it in the most efficient position relative to the pedal and crank, and therefore allowing a more efficient transfer of power. There is, of course, the usual bewildering variety of mutually incompatible makes and standards, but the best for everyday use (as opposed to high-performance racing) is Shimano's SPD, for which a wide variety of compatible shoes are available. These pedals have the advantage of being double-sided (so you can clip in whichever way up the pedal is) and robust. You can also walk normally in SPD-cleated shoes – not always the case with other systems.

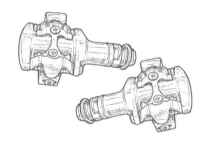

SPD-COMPATIBLE CLIPLESS PEDALS

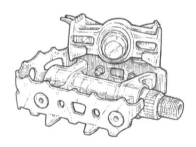

FLAT PEDALS

Flat (or platform) pedals

The kind of pedal that we all learned on, flat pedals are simple, light and cheap. Why would you want anything else? There is no reason not to use them unless you plan to ride competitively or for long distances. For short hops, errands around town and everyday use, plastic or metal flat pedals are fine – and don't let any snobs in Lycra tell you otherwise.

1.18 The toolbox

Thankfully, modern standardization of many components means that you need far fewer tools to build a bike than you used to. If you're working with a steel bike and new parts, a set of hex keys deals with most things. However, a few specialist tools for specialist jobs remain necessary.

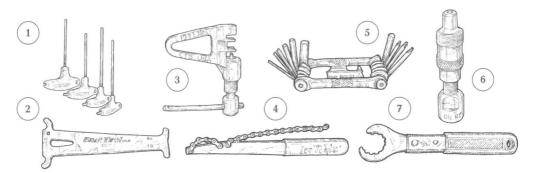

1 - Set of hex keys
You can get by with the hex keys (or Allen keys) that you get on a multitool, but it will be slower and less comfortable to use than a set of specialist hex keys, ideally with an ergonomic grip. You'll need a set including 2mm, 2.5mm, 3mm, 4mm, 5mm, 6mm and 8mm.

2 - Chain wear indicator
You won't need this for the build, but you need one in the toolbox so you can keep an eye on your chain as it stretches with use, and know when to change it.

3 - Chain tool
If you have a good multitool you may be able to get by without a dedicated chain tool (or chain-breaker), but they make life much easier – and you'll use it many times over the life of your bike.

4 - Chain whip
You need this when removing or fitting the cassette or freewheel.

5 - Multitool
If you've only ever used the cheap multitool that you were given for Christmas by a well-meaning relative who knows that you like bikes, you are probably sceptical as to this tool's usefulness. A low-quality one is horrible to use, flimsy, uncomfortable, and with hex keys so weak that they visibly flex when put under strain. However, a good-quality model, made of high-tensile steel and including hex keys, screwdrivers, spoke tensioners and a chain tool, is a joy. I've used a 17-function Crank Brothers model for many years; it is robust, light, and good for all manner of repairs out and about.

6 - Crank extractor
You'll need a crank extractor to repair, or service, a three-piece (square-pin) bottom bracket and the cranks and chainwheel that come with it. You will probably need one if you're restoring an older bike, but can do without if you're building from scratch.

7 - Bottom bracket wrench
You need to have the right tool for the bottom bracket that you intend to fit. Check what is required when you buy the bottom bracket. The tool won't be expensive: sometimes the same tool will fit for a disc brake lock ring, too.

Screwdrivers
Although the majority of modern components are held in place with hex bolts, you will still need a small cross-head screwdriver to adjust your derailleurs, while fittings such as a rack, lights or computer may require a flat-head screwdriver.

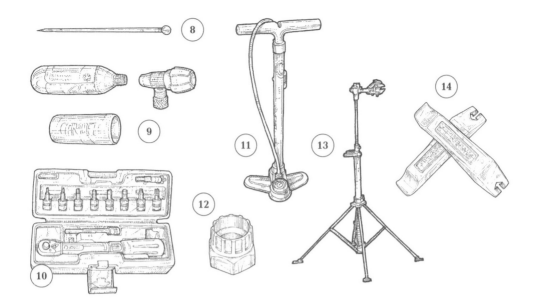

8 - Sharp point

Sometimes you just need something thin and pointed – to scrape gunk off your jockey wheels, perhaps, or clear the opening of a cable jacket before you thread new cable through it. I use a steel cocktail stick that has never held an olive in a martini, but has helped me out numerous times on builds, repairs and maintenance.

9 - CO_2 inflator cartridge and head

If you're fitting or running tubeless tyres, you will find this is the easiest way to inflate them in place (especially for the first time); the unit is small and light enough to warrant packing when you ride out, too. Filling a tyre in less than a second with high-pressure CO_2 is undeniably dramatic and convenient: be careful not to burn your fingers on the flash-frozen head, though – the boiling CO_2 rapidly cools the whole unit. CO_2 also seeps more rapidly than oxygen and nitrogen through the tyre's rubber walls, so you will need to top up the pressure with

atmospheric gas from a manual pump at intervals for a few days afterwards. And please don't be the idiot who leaves a used steel cartridge on a lovely rural pathway.

10 - Torque wrench

An absolute necessity if you are building up a carbon-fibre frame, a torque wrench tells you exactly how much force you are putting into tightening a bolt or component. This is crucial, as carbon fibre is vulnerable to the high forces that tools can exert, and over-tightening one bolt can write off an entire frame. Get a set that includes a complete range of hex (Allen), T25 and T30 heads, and an extension bar.

11 - Track pump with pressure gauge

An invaluable tool that has come down dramatically in price, a foot pump takes the sweat out of pumping your tyres up and lets you objectively judge the pressure at which you run your tyres.

12 - Cassette lockring tool

The cassette needs to be firmly tightened down. There isn't a standard tooth pattern for the tool you need for this, so make sure you have one to match the make and model of cassette that you choose.

13 - Workshop stand

This is not essential, but makes life easier and more comfortable, holding the bike at the right height for you to see what you're working on without bending, stretching awkwardly or sitting on the floor. Keeping the wheels in the air makes it much easier to fine-tune brakes and gears, too.

14 - Tyre levers

They're ugly, they're plastic, it's usually a pain to use them, but you need at least two. If you have a beautiful set of elegantly curved vintage steel levers, admire their finish and design, but do not use them to change a tyre: they are much more likely to put a hole through your inner tube and send you back to square one.

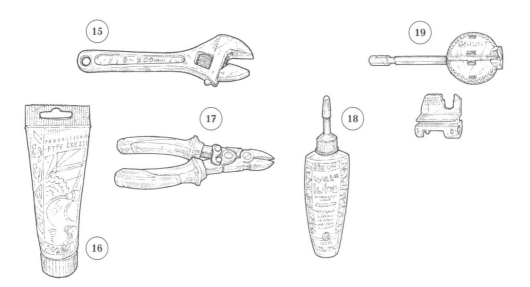

15 - Adjustable end wrench

You need this to apply torque to larger fixings including the cassette lockring, crank extractor and some bottom bracket cups. 200mm is long enough for a build; if you have to dismantle an old, rusted-up bike, you might appreciate the additional leverage that a hefty 300mm wrench will provide.

16 - Grease

A 100ml tube of PTFE grease will last you a while: use it wherever metal touches metal, or metal is unpainted, to prevent rusting and galvanic corrosion. This will make repairs and maintenance much easier and extend the bicycle's life considerably, particularly if your bike often gets wet. The exception is the drive train: grease on your chain, cassette or chainring will attract dirt and form a nasty gunk that quickly wears out moving parts. A good rule of thumb is to use grease in places that are out of sight, and a chain lubricant elsewhere.

17 - Wirecutters

Cables, and cable housings, are made of steel, and you need a dedicated tool to cut them cleanly. Pliers or pincers will not work.

18 - Chain lubricant

There are many brands of chain lubricant, all of which have their fans: broadly speaking, 'dry' lube is better if you ride in good weather (it needs to be reapplied if your chain gets wet); 'wet' lube is preferable if you are an all-weather cyclist. The actual brand you use is less important than applying it regularly and keeping the chain as clean as you can.

19 - Spoke keys

To tighten or loosen the spokes on your wheel you need a key that has the same profile as the spoke's nipple. Spoke keys come in many different shapes and sizes, but all work the same way. Some wheelmakers supply a key with each set of wheels; some multitools have a selection of keys on them.

What tools do you really need?

I'm working on the assumption that you don't want to spend money on tools that you will only use once or twice, and that you don't already have your own fully equipped workshop. There are a couple of jobs that you may want to ask the professionals at a bike workshop to carry out, simply because they demand specific tools that, if you buy, you'll only need to use once. Fortunately, these jobs (fitting bearing cups and cutting steerer tubing to the right length) happen right at the beginning and end of the build, so you don't have to interrupt yourself with repeated visits to bike shops. Apart from those jobs, a fairly small selection of tools will get you through the build and a subsequent lifetime of maintenance.

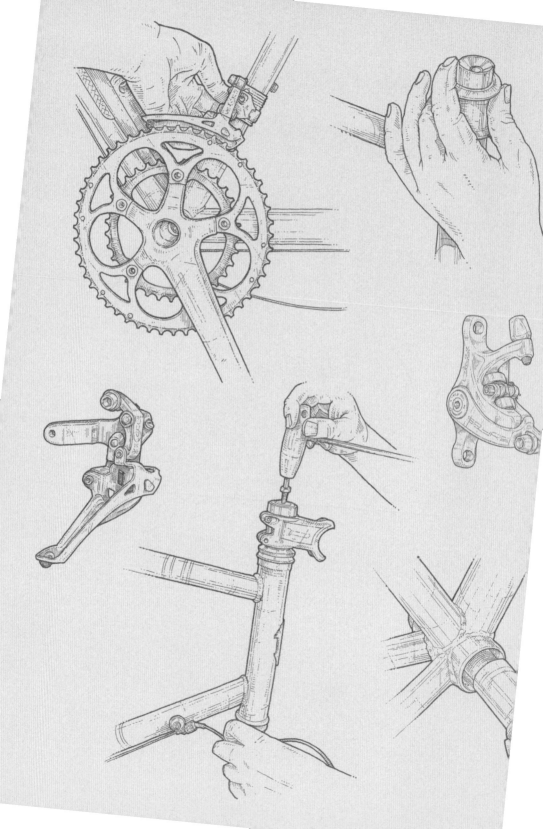

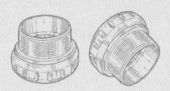

2
The Build
DAY ONE

So, you've got the tools, you've got a pile of components, and you've got the weekend ahead of you. It's going to be one of the most productive you'll ever spend – and will give you a lifetime's riding joy. Starting with the robust junctions of the headset and bottom bracket, you'll lay the foundations of the bike. When they are in place, you'll add handlebars, shifters and brake levers, and route the cables to the brakes and derailleurs. Finally, you'll fit tyres to the wheels.

2.1 Your workspace and getting started

Your workspace should be well lit and large enough to accommodate the whole bike on your stand. Lay the tools out where you can get at them easily, along with a rag for wiping grease off your fingers. Have a couple of small containers ready for the various loose bolts, washers and bearings that will otherwise try to escape. And line up some music!

It is best to clamp the bike's seatpost, not any of the frame tubes, into the stand. This minimizes the risk of damage to delicate tubing – which is only a slight risk, but expensive if it occurs. The first thing you need to do is put the saddle on the seatpost, and the seatpost into the frame.

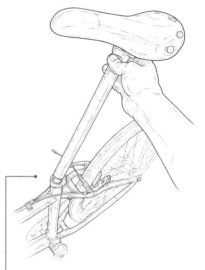

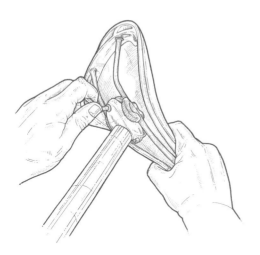

Fitting the saddle

The top of the seatpost has a fitting for the saddle. These vary in pattern, but usually have a clamp, held in place by two hex bolts, that grip the saddle's two rails and allows the saddle to be adjusted front to back and angled appropriately. Lightly grease the bolts and the inside surfaces of the clamp, then fit the saddle rails in and tighten so the saddle is firmly in place.

Fitting the seatpost

This is a simple job: loosen the bolt holding the seatpost clamp, lightly grease the post (with metal frames this is crucial to prevent seatpost and seat tube corroding together and becoming permanently bonded) and slide the post in. Tighten the seatpost clamp again. You need a good length of seatpost inside the seat tube. It should extend inside by at least twice the diameter of the seatpost, or 40mm past the joint of the top tube and the seat tube – whichever is longer.

The last section of the book will help you set the saddle height more exactly and make fine adjustments; see page 108.

Now place the frame in the stand, with the clamp holding the seatpost firmly and vertically.

2.2 Fitting the bottom bracket

Nearly invisible at the bottom of your frame, and playing a very simple, unglamorous role in how your bike works, the bottom bracket (BB for short) is easy to forget about. It is, however, incredibly important: all the effort you put into your riding will be transmitted via the BB, so it is crucial that it is well fitted and healthy, and is compatible with your frame's bottom bracket shell — the opening in your frame designed to house it.

There is a frankly baffling variety of bottom brackets out there, but most follow one of two basic patterns, as described below.

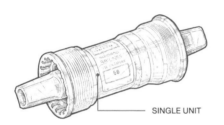

SINGLE UNIT

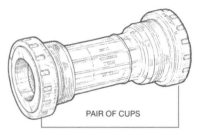

PAIR OF CUPS

Three-piece or cartridge BB

This is a chunky unit that includes the built-in axle around which your cranks will turn. The axle protrudes from each end, and has a tapering square cross-section to which you attach the crank arm on the left, and the crank plus chainring unit on the right side – hence, 'three-piece'. Your crankset must be 'square-taper' to work with a three-piece BB.

External bearing cup or thru-spindle BB

These units come in two parts, one fitted into each side of the bottom bracket. They do not include an axle. With this kind of set-up, the axle is connected to the cranks directly and merely passes snugly through the BB. This allows the axle, and the bearings, to be lighter and stronger, so high-end BBs (including the ranges of Campagnolo, Shimano and SRAM) are now all in this basic pattern. Another advantage is ease of fitting, maintenance and replacement. Your crankset must include an axle if it is to be compatible with external bearing cups.

How to fit a three-piece or cartridge BB

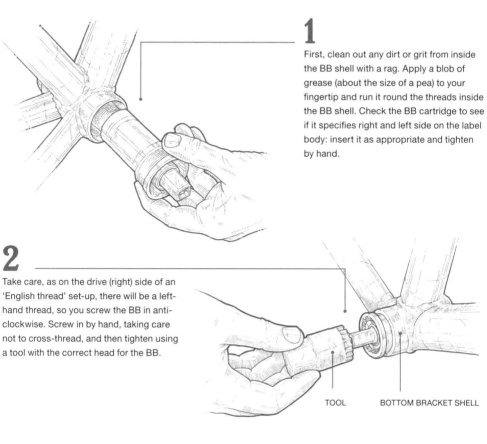

1

First, clean out any dirt or grit from inside the BB shell with a rag. Apply a blob of grease (about the size of a pea) to your fingertip and run it round the threads inside the BB shell. Check the BB cartridge to see if it specifies right and left side on the label body: insert it as appropriate and tighten by hand.

2

Take care, as on the drive (right) side of an 'English thread' set-up, there will be a left-hand thread, so you screw the BB in anti-clockwise. Screw in by hand, taking care not to cross-thread, and then tighten using a tool with the correct head for the BB.

TOOL   BOTTOM BRACKET SHELL

3

A smaller, threaded ring goes into the other side of the BB shell. Tighten this by hand initially, then use the wrench.

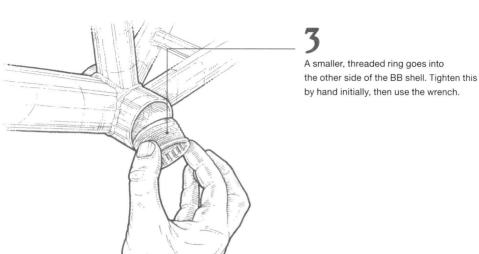

How to fit external bearing cups

1

If the bearing cups are compatible with your frame, fitting them is simple. First, clean out any dirt or grit from the inside of the BB shell with a rag. Apply a blob of grease (about the size of a pea) to your fingertip and run it round the threads inside the BB shell.

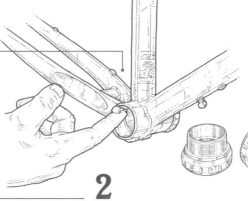

2

The BB consists of two sets of bearings and, sometimes, a plastic tube that holds them together, and spacers that sit between the BB and the frame and ensure that the axle on the crankset will be a perfect fit. Each half will have its side (R or L) stamped on it, as well as an arrow showing the direction of the thread: check this, as on the drive (right) side of an 'English thread' set-up, this will be left-hand, so you screw the BB in anti-clockwise. On the left side, the thread is normal.

Taking care not to cross-thread, screw both in by hand with the plastic tube (if there is one) inserted into one (the other part will meet with it inside the BB shell), fitting the spacers, if included, between the bearings and the frame. (If spacers – thin, steel rings – are included, fit them: if you don't need them, you can easily remove them when you fit the crankset.)

3

Tighten firmly using the bottom bracket wrench.

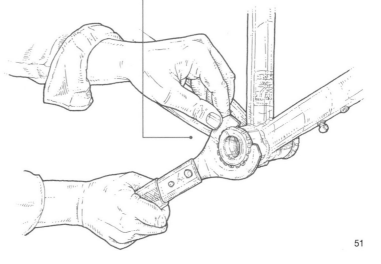

2.3 Crankset

The crankset has to be compatible with the bottom bracket, fitting perfectly so that it turns without wobbles or resistance, and transfers all the power of your pedal stroke through to the chain.

In most modern groupsets, the spindle is an integral part of the drive-side crank: it passes through the bottom bracket (a thru-spindle model) and is bolted to the left-side crank. With three-piece designs (more common on older bikes), the two cranks are fitted separately to the spindle that is part of the BB (bottom bracket) unit.

Fitting a thru-spindle crankset

CHAINRING

SPINDLE

CRANK

1

Lightly grease the spindle, and pass it through the bottom bracket from the drive side. You may need to encourage it with a rubber mallet (or a heavy book) if there is resistance.

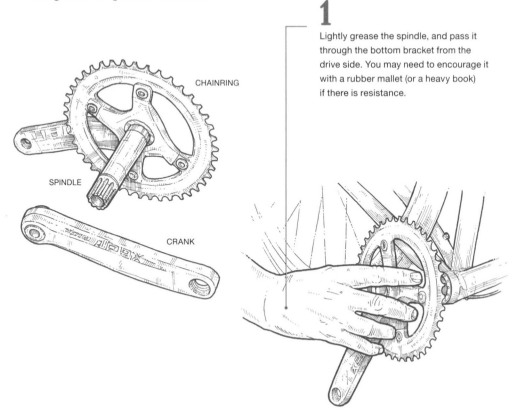

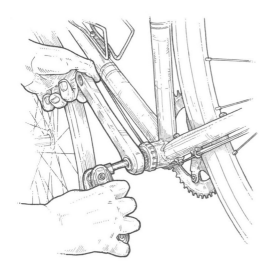

2

Fit and tighten the other crank arm and firmly tighten the bolt that holds it to the spindle.

It is important to check that the cranks rotate smoothly and that they aren't loose. If there is side-to-side movement, then the spindle is too long for the space allowed for it by the BB. This is easily remedied by adding spacers (narrow rings) between the BB and the frame's BB shell: remove the spindle, remove the BB, add one spacer on each side, replace and try again. If the cranks are too tight (gripping the BB tightly), you should remove one spacer.

Fitting crank arms to a three-piece bottom bracket

Most spindles on three-piece BBs are made to one of three standards: square-tapered, Shimano's Octalink standard (which has eight splines – notches – on the end of the spindle), or the ISIS Drive (which has ten splines). These are not mutually compatible, so the cranks must match the spindle, but they are all fitted in a similar way.

1

If you have a splined spindle, put a dab of grease around the splines on either side. Square-tapered spindles don't need grease. Place the drive-side crank onto the right side of the spindle, and lightly grease and thread in the bolt.

2

Tighten the bolt – it needs to firmly anchor the crank arm around the spindle. On the other side, fit the left arm so it points 180 degrees away from the right arm, and repeat the process. There may be dust caps to fit over the bolts: if so, lightly grease the threads and install. Check that the crank arms are firmly in place and there is no wobble before proceeding.

2.4 Fitting the headset and fork crown

If you are building up a second-hand or ex-display frame, it is very likely that the headset races (in the frame) and crown race (on the fork) are already fitted, in which case, move on to page 57.

However, if you're building up a new frame, they will need fitting. This requires a couple of tools that you won't use much (possibly never again), so you should consider asking your local bike shop to do the job before the build proper.

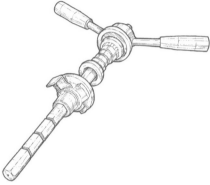

A purpose-built headset press is a big, heavy, expensive tool.

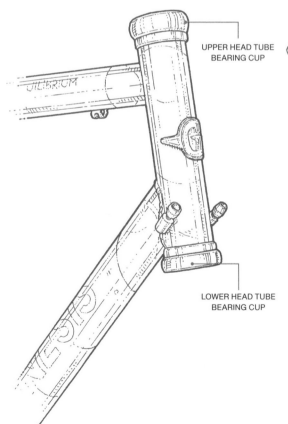

UPPER HEAD TUBE BEARING CUP

LOWER HEAD TUBE BEARING CUP

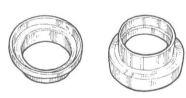

The narrow side of each bearing cup is pressed into the frame tubing, leaving the flared sides to either hold single unit closed bearings, or a set of loose bearings.

Fitting headset cups

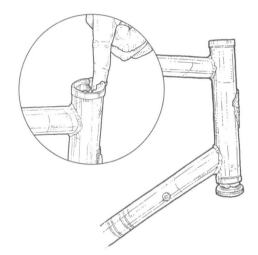

1

You will need a headset press and two correctly sized bearing cups. Place the frame into your stand so that the head tube is at chest height, then wipe a dab of grease inside the head tube's top and bottom edges.

2

Remove the bottom of the headset press. Place the cups on the ends of the head tube (make sure that you have them the right way round) and place the press through the head tube, with the handles at the top and the stepped ring of the press aligned on the top cup. Replace the other stepped ring and the end of the press underneath the bottom cup, and tighten until press and cup meet.

TIP: If you don't want to spend money on a special tool, yet want to fit the headset yourself, there are two ways to proceed. First, it is possible to fit a headset using brute force – a hammer – and a block of wood to control the impact. This is only recommended for confident hammer-swingers who don't mind risking damage to headset, frame and self-esteem if things don't go according to plan. A less dramatic method is to make your own headset press using simple hardware components: many cheap DIY sets are listed on eBay.

3

Make sure that the cups are aligned evenly on the ends of the tube and sitting neatly on the stepped rings, then start to tighten the handles on the top until both cups are pressed firmly and evenly into the frame. They should be flush with the end of the tube all the way round.

2.5 Fitting the fork crown race

The crown race sits snugly on the forks: the bearings sit between it and the lower headset cup. Some crown races are split: fit these by hand, sliding them down the steerer tube. Crown rings that are complete rings fit tightly around the steerer, and need to be tapped down using a tool and a hammer. The tool you need, the crown race setter, won't be used much, so consider asking your local bike shop to do the job.

1

Apply some grease around the protrusion at the base of the steerer tube, where the race will sit, and slide the crown race, flat side downwards, onto it.

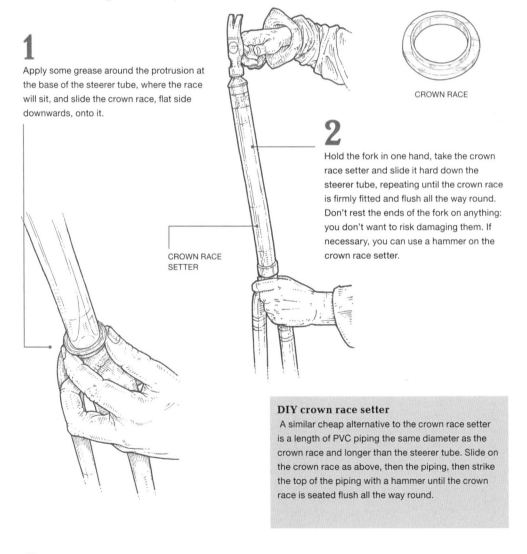

CROWN RACE

CROWN RACE SETTER

2

Hold the fork in one hand, take the crown race setter and slide it hard down the steerer tube, repeating until the crown race is firmly fitted and flush all the way round. Don't rest the ends of the fork on anything: you don't want to risk damaging them. If necessary, you can use a hammer on the crown race setter.

DIY crown race setter

A similar cheap alternative to the crown race setter is a length of PVC piping the same diameter as the crown race and longer than the steerer tube. Slide on the crown race as above, then the piping, then strike the top of the piping with a hammer until the crown race is seated flush all the way round.

2.6 Fitting forks with a threadless headset and a separate stem

With the crown race and headset race fitted into the head tube of the frame, and the crown race fitted on the fork, you're now able to fit the forks, held in place by the two headset bearings that let you steer freely, confident that the bike will stay in one piece. If your frame and fork already have the bearings fitted, great — pick up these instructions at Step 4 to fit the stem.

1

Put the frame upright into the stand with the head tube at about waist height and lightly grease the inside of the bearing cups in the top and bottom of the head tube. Place the bearings into the head cup. Make sure that you fit them the right way up: closed bearings (in which you can't see the ball bearings) will have a profile that fits it snugly into the cup.

If the bearings are open (and you can see the ball bearings), place them with the flat side of their retaining cage facing upwards. You must grease open bearings – use a small blob, as big as a pea, and work it around the ball bearings with a fingertip. An open race may also have a small rubber ring for a dust seal: place it on top of the bearings.

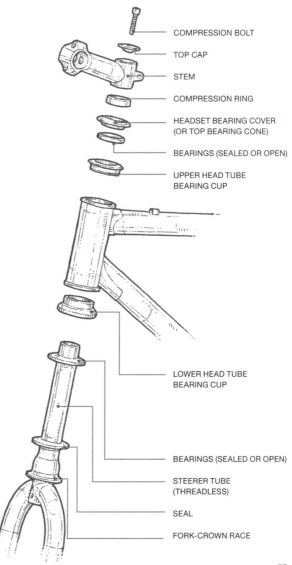

COMPRESSION BOLT

TOP CAP

STEM

COMPRESSION RING

HEADSET BEARING COVER
(OR TOP BEARING CONE)

BEARINGS (SEALED OR OPEN)

UPPER HEAD TUBE
BEARING CUP

LOWER HEAD TUBE
BEARING CUP

BEARINGS (SEALED OR OPEN)

STEERER TUBE
(THREADLESS)

SEAL

FORK-CROWN RACE

2

Now turn to the crown race bearing. Grease the fork crown race, and very lightly grease the whole length of the tube (even the lightest coating will impede corrosion). If you have closed bearings, slide them over the steerer tube, making sure that they are the right way up to fit snugly into the lower head-tube bearing cup.

If they are open bearings, then grease them as you did with the upper set, and place them directly into the lower head-tube bearing cup so that the flat side of the ring faces outwards, then apply the dust seal. Both will be held in place by the grease.

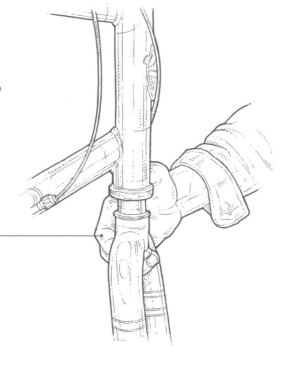

3

Carefully pass the steerer through the headtube so it sticks out at the top and the fork crown race is flush with the bearings in the lower cup. Holding the forks with one hand, place the headset bearing cover (or top bearing cone) over the steerer tube and press it down onto the headset bearing to seal the whole unit.

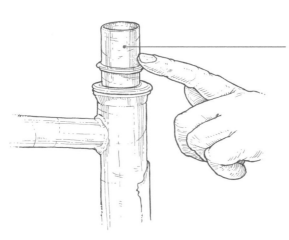

4

The unit may have a separate compression ring to hold it tight to the steerer tube. If so, fit this over the steerer tube and press it into place – you shouldn't need to use force. The forks should now be gripped in the head tube and you can let go of them.

5

There will be a length of bare steerer tube at the top of the unit: this is where you will fit the stem and, if necessary, spacers. You can adjust the height of the stem (using spacers placed either above or below it) according to what is most comfortable for you after you've had a few rides; for now, just fit the stem so you can proceed with the build. Loosen the two hex bolts at the back of the stem and slide it onto the steerer tube. If some bare tube projects above it, add one or more spacers above or below until the top of the steerer is hidden inside them, and about 3mm recessed.

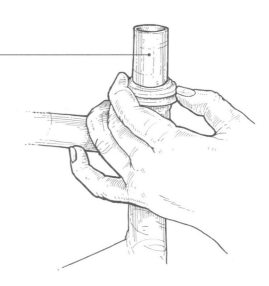

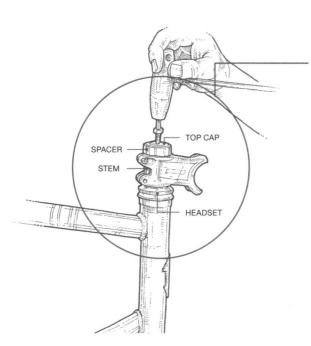

TOP CAP

SPACER

STEM

HEADSET

6

Replace the top cap, then lightly grease the compression bolt. Using a hex key, tighten the bolt through the hole in the middle of the top cap. It will engage with the thread inside, pulling the top cap tight. At the same time, press the fork upwards from below so that the crown race is definitely engaged. As the compression bolt tightens, it will press the top cap onto the spacers and stem and tighten up both bearings. Don't over-tighten it – the forks should rotate smoothly, without resistance, and this is easily fine-tuned later on. Finally, tighten the hex bolts on the stem, making sure that it is facing forwards as you do.

2.7 Fitting threaded forks and a quill stem

It's unlikely that you'll be fitting threaded forks if you are building a new bike from scratch, but if you are restoring or rebuilding an old frame and fork, it may have them. This was the standard for many years and is still used on many cheaper or traditional city bikes.

It has the advantage of flexibility in use: it is easy and quick to raise or drop a quill stem to a new height. Set against this is additional weight, and the need to remove, clean and regrease the stem occasionally so that it doesn't seize up. The fork steerer also has to be cut to the right length for its head tube – which is not an issue if you are restoring an existing frame-and-fork pairing.

1

Fix the frame upright into the stand with the head tube at waist height and lightly grease the insides of the head tube bearing cups. Place the bearings into the head cup. Bearings can either be open or sealed: in an open bearing, the balls are held in place by a light metal retainer, and you can see the ball bearings. Make sure that you fit them the right way up: closed bearings will have a profile that fits them snugly into the cup.

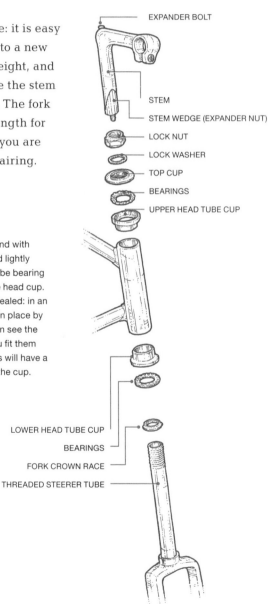

EXPANDER BOLT

STEM

STEM WEDGE (EXPANDER NUT)

LOCK NUT

LOCK WASHER

TOP CUP

BEARINGS

UPPER HEAD TUBE CUP

LOWER HEAD TUBE CUP

BEARINGS

FORK CROWN RACE

THREADED STEERER TUBE

2

Now turn to the crown race bearing. Grease the fork crown race, and very lightly grease the whole length of the tube and its thread. If you have closed bearings, slide them over the steerer tube, making sure that they fit snugly into the lower head tube cup. If they are open bearings, grease them as you did with the upper set, and place them into the cup so that the flat side of the retainer faces outwards, then apply the dust seal. Both will be held in place by the grease.

3

Carefully pass the steerer through the head tube so it sticks out at the top, and the lower head tube cup and fork crown race grip the bearings at the bottom. Holding the forks with one hand, screw the top cup down (with your fingers) until it is flush with the upper head tube cup.

If you have open bearings, this is when you need to experiment slightly: if the top cup is screwed down too tightly, steering will be stiff and there will be a grinding feeling. If it is too loose, the fork will wobble. Try loosening and tightening by slight increments, and rotate the forks to feel for smoothness. When you're happy, place the lock washer over the steerer tube, then screw down the lock nut using a spanner or adjustable end wrench, taking care not to tighten the headset cup at the same time.

If the bearings are a sealed unit, all you have to do is tighten the top cup with your fingers so that it is snug and there's no wobble, then place the washer over the steerer tube, then screw down the locknut on top using a spanner or adjustable end wrench. If the steerer tube extends more than a few millimetres above the locknut, then the excess length needs to be cut off with a hacksaw.

4

With the fork firmly in place, take the quill stem. Grease the bottom part of the stem, the stem wedge (expander nut) at the bottom, and the expander bolt that holds them together. With the stem wedge loose, insert the stem into the steerer tube, then tighten the expander bolt at the top until the stem wedge grips the stem firmly in place inside the steerer tube. You will adjust the height later.

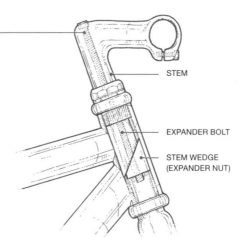

STEM

EXPANDER BOLT

STEM WEDGE (EXPANDER NUT)

2.8 Fitting handlebars to the stem

Whatever shape you have chosen, handlebars are simple to fit to either quill stems or separate stems. However, the diameter of the bar at the centre (where the stem grips it) has to match the opening that will receive it on the front end of the stem.

If you're using second-hand bars with sticky traces of old adhesive, it is a good idea to clean them up now using adhesive cleaner and a sponge or scouring pad. Most bars have small marks in the centre allowing you to align them symmetrically – identify these before you start.

Fitting bars to a quill stem

Loosen the bolt on the underside using a hex key (or small wrench, depending on the head of the bolt) so that the aperture at the end opens up enough to admit the bar. Lightly grease the thread of the bolt. Thread the bar through, jiggling it as you get to the curves, until it is centred and horizontal. Tighten the bolt up as firmly as possible to prevent the bars rotating.

Fitting bars to a separate stem

Remove the front plate using a hex key to loosen the four bolts, grease them lightly, then hold the centre of the bars into the curve of the front of the stem, place the front plate of the stem back and reattach using the bolts. Don't tighten them all the way at first: make sure that the handlebars are centred exactly, and horizontal, before tightening the bolts firmly to prevent the bars rotating.

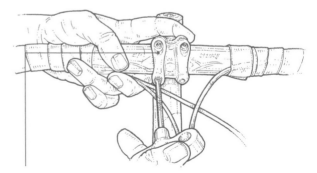

The first two bolts should be diagonally opposite each other. Tighten them alternately to ensure equal loading at top and bottom of the front plate.

2.9 Fitting shifters and brake levers to drop handlebars

Now the handlebars are in place, it's time to fit the brake levers and gear shifters. If you have drop handlebars, these will probably be in a pair of integrated units. The fitting bolt and the entry points for brake and gear cables will be hidden under a protective rubber hood.

For many years, gear levers were located on the down tube, so every time you shifted gear you had to reach down, letting go of the handlebar as you did so. Fortunately, these days, nearly all gear changes are actuated by levers, rotating grips or switches on the handlebars, making changing quicker, safer and more reliable.

A new integrated shifter may be supplied with a bare steel cable running out of it: this is the gear cable. Keep it wound up in a loop for now. To fit integrated shifters on drop bars, roll the top side of the rubber hood up until the head of a hex (or possibly a P25) bolt is revealed underneath. This tightens or loosens the metal band that grips the shifters onto the bar.

Loosen it a couple of turns anti-clockwise, then thread the band around the end of the bars (checking that the shifter is on the correct side) and work them up until they are nearly at the top. Tighten in place using the same bolt. You adjust the exact positioning later, but this will let you fit gears and brakes in the meantime.

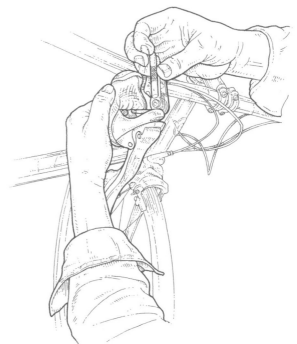

2.10 Fitting shifters and brake levers to flat handlebars

Flat handlebars are much easier to manage than drop bars: the brake and gear levers slide on easily, and you don't need to worry about bar tape. Fittings vary, so identify the bolt that tightens the handles into place before you slide them onto the bar.

1

Make sure that the handlebars are firmly gripped in the stem, and fitted symmetrically. Most bars have an indicator showing the exact centre which you can use to line them up.

2

Identify the left and right side shifters and brake levers, and locate the mounting bolts on your brake levers and gear shifters.

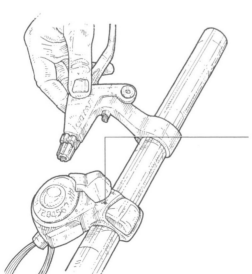

3

If the gear shifter is a separate trigger-style unit, then slide it over the handlebar tube first, then the brake lever, then fit the grip. Grips are often difficult to slide on: hairspray is an effective clean lubricant for them – spray some inside the grips and fit them quickly before it evaporates.

4

If the gear shifter is a separate
twist shifter, fit it after the brake lever,
so that it sits inside it.

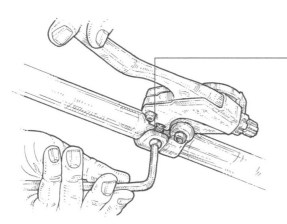

5

Make sure that the grip is firmly on, then
tighten up the brake levers and gear shifters
so that they are comfortably aligned for the
position of your hands. Usually, you should
leave some space between the inside ends
of the grips and the levers: there may be a
spacer (narrow ring) to make this easier. You
should point the brake levers downwards
by about 45 degrees, so your fingers reach
comfortably around them.

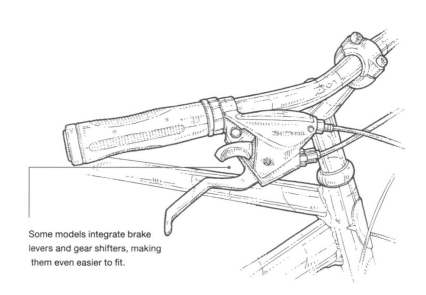

Some models integrate brake
levers and gear shifters, making
them even easier to fit.

2.11 The brakes

As discussed on page 26, what sort of brakes you have is determined by the fittings on the frame. Here, we'll look at the two most popular kinds: disc brakes and rim brakes.

Whichever type you're using, you will fine-tune them later, when the wheels are in place, but fitting them will let you run the cables down and connect the callipers to their levers.

Fitting disc brake callipers

Disc brakes are bolted onto special fittings on the frame and fork, and work by applying pressure to a metal rotor (the disc, which we will come to later) that is mounted at the centre of the wheel. A set of callipers is mounted on the frame (which grip the rotor when actuated) and is connected by a cable to the levers mounted on your handlebars. Lightly grease the mounting bolts and use them to fit the callipers to the mounts. Don't tighten them fully: there needs to be a little lateral movement when you come to tune the brakes later on.

Rotors are available in four sizes, 140mm, 160mm, 180mm or 200mm in diameter. The size that you need is determined by the position of the mounts on your frame, so check what you need before purchase.

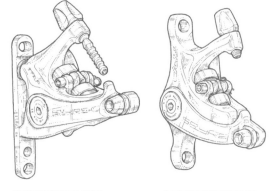

FLAT-MOUNT CALLIPER   POST-MOUNT CALLIPER

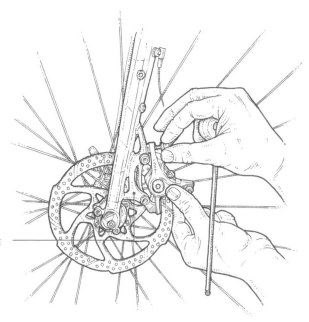

POST-MOUNT BRAKE
CALLIPER UNIT
ON A FRONT FORK

Fitting rim brake callipers

Rim brake callipers are mounted on bolts that pass through holes in the frame and fork: they work by pressing rubber brake blocks onto the rim of the wheel from both sides.

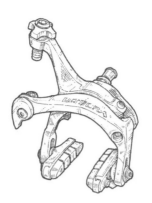

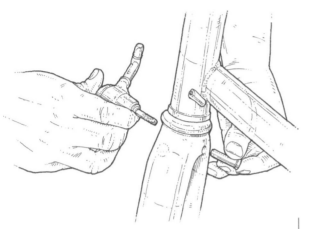

1

The front unit has a bolt that goes into a hole on the fork, just below the crown. Lightly grease the bolt before feeding it in.

2

A recessed nut meets the bolt: tighten it firmly using a hex key. Repeat the process for the rear unit, where the equivalent bolt passes through a hole in the brake bridge, between the seat stays.

Hydraulic brake systems

In recent years hydraulically actuated disc brake systems have appeared on the market and are now offered by the major component manufacturers at the higher end of their ranges. These work on a different principle: the brake callipers are closed not by a cable being pulled, but by hydraulic fluid being forced along sealed hoses. They are more expensive and difficult to set up than cable-actuated models, and of most interest to performance-oriented cyclists, so aren't covered in this book.

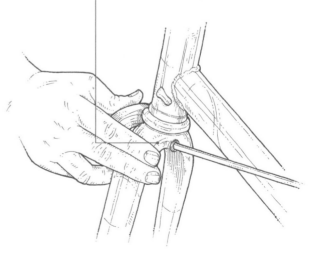

2.12 Front derailleur

Most groupsets include a front derailleur, which moves the chain between two or three cogs on the front crank, giving more range to your selection of gears.

The cage of the front derailleur (or front mech) holds the chain, and moves in and out relative to its position on the seat tube, pushing the chain so that its links engage with chainrings of different sizes. Increasing the tension on the cable pushes the cage outwards and the chain onto the largest ring, resulting in a higher gearing. Reduce the tension on the cable and the cage pulls back inwards, so the chain drops down onto the smaller ring, resulting in a lower gearing. This gear change only works if the chain and chainrings are moving, so you cannot change gear while stopped.

Most front mechs work well with a variety of chains and shifters, so there are fewer compatibility issues than with rear mechs. A triple chain ring does require a dedicated triple front mech, which will have a larger plate on the inner side of the cage.

Front derailleurs come in two types: band-on or braze-on. Your choice is determined by your frame. Band-on (or clamp-on) mechs have a clamp that binds them firmly to the seat tube, so you need to double-check that the diameter of the seat tube matches the diameter of the clamp. Braze-on fittings are all to a common standard so compatibility is not an issue.

Your chainring (and, therefore, your bottom bracket and crankset) need to be in place before you fit the derailleur, as its positioning on the seat tube depends on the diameter of the largest ring.

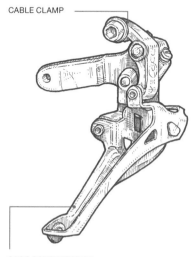

CABLE CLAMP

CAGE CONSISTING OF
OUTER AND INNER PLATES

Braze-on mechs

These mechs are bolted onto a permanent fitting on the frame. Don't worry, you don't have to do any brazing to install them – they should really be called 'bolt-on'.

The mount for a braze-on mech will allow for the derailleur to be mounted at different heights. Bolt the mech to the mount and finger-tighten it so that it stays in place. Then move the mech so that the outer edge of the cage is about 2mm above the points of the biggest ring, and tighten the bolt on the clamp with a hex key.

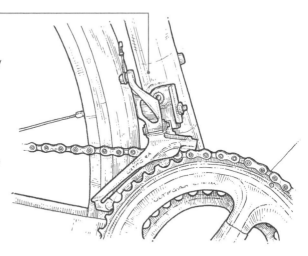

Band-on mechs

With a band-on mech, fit the clamp around the seat tube and finger-tighten it so that it stays in place. Then position the mech so that the outer edge of the cage is about 2mm above the points of the biggest ring and tighten the bolt on the clamp with a hex key.

The curve of the cage should match the curve of the chainring. Some new mechs come with a sticker on the cage that guides you to the best position.

2.13 Rear derailleur

Of all of the bicycle's components, the rear derailleur is perhaps the most ingenious. With a tiny, carefully judged side-to-side movement of the chain, at a point where it isn't under load, the rear mech can instantly transform the way your effort hits the rear wheel, allowing you to grind up a hill or speed down it.

A modern gearing system uses the shifter to make precise adjustments to the length of a cable that connects shifter and derailleur. The derailleur makes equally precise movements in turn, pushing the chain from sprocket to sprocket on the cassette. The basics of the system have been unchanged for decades, and refined to the point where a tiny movement of your finger on the shifter will reliably and instantly move you up or down the gears. This precision makes two demands. First, the derailleur's cage has to be long enough to cope with the range of gears on your cassette. A wide range, with large sprockets in the low gears, needs a derailleur with a long cage. Second, you need to tune today's sensitive rear mechs with care.

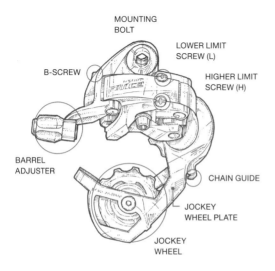

MOUNTING BOLT

LOWER LIMIT SCREW (L)

B-SCREW

HIGHER LIMIT SCREW (H)

BARREL ADJUSTER

CHAIN GUIDE

JOCKEY WHEEL PLATE

JOCKEY WHEEL

Rear mechs vary in design but feature the same essential ingredients. Before you fit your mech, make sure that you can identify the mounting bolt, the high and low limit screws (often labelled H and L), the b-screw (or body-angle screw) underneath the mounting bolt (if there is one: some mechs do without), the mounting bolt tab (if there is no b-screw), the cable clamp and the barrel adjuster. The two jockey wheels guide the chain through the derailleur: note also the chain guide, under which the chain is threaded.

Fitting the rear derailleur

The rear mech is fitted directly to the hanger. This is either part of the frame (extending below the dropout on the drive side, usually on a steel frame) or a separate piece of aluminium that is bolted to the frame at the point where chainstays and seatstays meet. Pictured is the integrated hanger on a steel frame. Note the hanger tab on the bottom.

HANGER TAB

Derailleur hangers

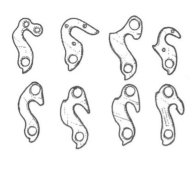

There are hundreds of different models of derailleur hanger: if your frame needs one, but doesn't have one with it (as may be the case if you are working with a second-hand frame), you will need to source a replacement carefully. There are online specialists who can help you with this.

Place the frame in the stand at a comfortable working height. If you have a separate hanger, fit it carefully, lightly greasing the fixing bolts and the surface between the frame's dropout and the hanger before bolting it tightly on.

Now take the rear derailleur. Lightly grease the thread on the mounting bolt. Next to the bolt there will be either a tab or the b-screw. This must press against the corresponding tab on the bottom of

the derailleur hanger; rotate the derailleur clockwise until it does. Then, with a hex key, thread the mounting bolt carefully into the hanger, and tighten.

Ensure that you aren't cross-threading the mounting bolt in (if you feel any resistance, stop, unscrew and try again) and that the b-screw sits behind the hanger tab. Tighten until the mech is flush against the hanger.

2.14 Laying cables

Now the handlebars, derailleur and brake callipers are in place, it is time to connect one to the other. There are various small, fiddly pieces to deal with now, so get a pot ready to keep them in, or use the magnetic tray on your work stand, if there is one.

Both brake cables and gear cables work on the same principle. A steel cable is directed through a steel housing that can't be compressed. When the cable is pulled at one end, it retracts by exactly the same amount at the other. Because the cable housing is flexible, this force can be threaded around the bike, changing direction as necessary. This mechanism is beautifully adaptable and forgiving, but it does demand that all cable housings are securely fitted at both ends.

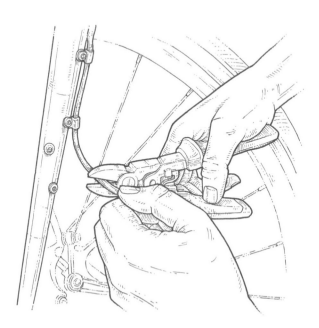

You'll need a pair of wirecutters: both cable housings and cables are tough, and you need to cut them cleanly. Pliers will not work.

Depending on your brake and gear set-up, this is how much cabling you'll require (these are generous measurements based on an extra-large frame, so you should have a few centimeters spare).

BRAKE CABLE	
For disc brakes	90cm (front) + 160cm (rear) = 250cm
For rim brakes	20+50cm (rear) + 50cm (front) = 120cm

GEAR CABLE	
Front derailleur	60cm (into shifter)
Rear derailleur	60cm (into shifter) + 30cm (into mech) = 90cm
	Total = 150cm

Internal gear cable routing

Many modern carbon-fibre and aluminium frames feature internal cable routing, which hides cables away inside the frame's tubing. The entry and exit points have plastic cable routers, against which cable housings press: arrangements vary significantly from frame to frame, so I will not attempt to cover them in this book. It does neaten up a bicycle's lines, but many people find routing cables this way frustrating. If your build involves internal routing, refer to the frame manufacturer's instructions, and equip yourself with a small metal hook to fish cables out of the apertures in the frame.

You'll also need enough cable housing for both the brake cables and the gear cables. Note that gear and brake cable housings are not the same diameter, and are differently constructed internally: brake cable housings are stronger, to deal with the forces being applied by the lever, whereas gear cable housings are built to be compressionless, making them more appropriate for the more precise, less forceful, movements of the gear cables. This is why brake cable housings are slightly greater in diameter than gear cable housings. Ferrules (small caps made of metal or plastic) are placed over their ends in order to prevent the cable housing splaying in use.

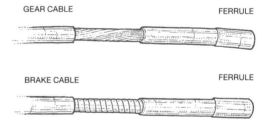

GEAR CABLE   FERRULE

BRAKE CABLE   FERRULE

TIP: Take care to avoid splaying the ends of your cables by forcing them into and through the housings. If one of the threads of the steel cable comes loose, you may be able to carefully wind it back on, but if the whole cable ends up like this, you'll need to cut it back and start again – if you have enough of the cable left.

Fitting gear cables

Highlighted in orange is the route your gear cabling should follow. Gear shifters sometimes arrive with the steel cable emerging from their base, already fitted. If so, skip Steps 2 and 3 on this page. Double check that you have the (thinner) gear cable housing to hand, not brake cable housing.

NOTE: most new cable housings have Teflon liners that do not require lubrication.

1

Fit the cable guide to the underside of the bottom bracket shell. It will need to route up to three cables, depending on your set-up: front derailleur, rear derailleur and rear disc brake. (The example pictured doesn't have a disc brake cable.)

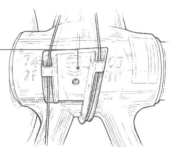

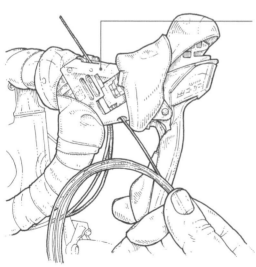

2

If the cable has not already been fitted to the shifter, you will need to thread it through. First, set the shifter to the setting that correlates to the derailleur being over the smallest sprocket (lowest tension). There will be a small hole on the underside of the shifter, underneath the rubber grip (refer to the manual to locate this). Taking care not to splay the end of the cable, thread it through this hole; it will pop out of its housing at the bars.

3

Take that end and gently pull the cable through the housing until the cylindrical head disappears into the bottom of the shifter. Check that this has engaged properly by holding the cable while you operate the shift lever. You should feel a pull on the cable as the lever works the shifter's ratchet mechanism. If it is working, return the shifter to the lowest tension setting before you continue.

4

One piece of housing connects the rear derailleur to the cable guide on the chainstay. To cut it to the right length, take the gear cable housing and hold one end in the barrel adjuster on the derailleur. Then curve it up and forward to the cable guide on the chainstay, making sure that the housing does not curve too tightly – this will impede the free movement of the cable and rear derailleur. Cut the housing at this point (the piece will be around 30cm long, depending on the location of the cable guide and derailleur) and use a sharp point to clear the opening at each end. Place a ferrule over each end, then seat the cable housing in the cable guide on the chainstay and the barrel adjuster on the derailleur, where it should remain in place.

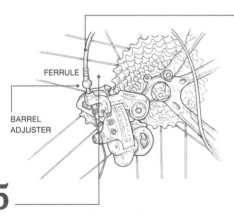

FERRULE

BARREL ADJUSTER

5

There may be a small rubber sheath to stop a dirty cable carrying gunk into the cable housing: slide it onto the cable, then thread the cable into the housing so it emerges at the derailleur. Pass it through the cable-fixing bolt and leave it for now – we'll come back to it when it's time to adjust the derailleur.

6

The second length of gear cable housing steers the cable from your shifters to the cable boss on the down tube. If you're fitting both front and rear derailleurs then you will use cable bosses on both sides; if just a rear derailleur, then only the boss on the right side of the tube.

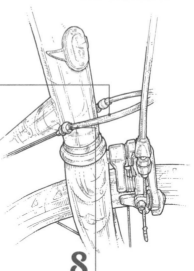

7

Hold one end of the cable at the shifter and use your other hand to run it along the handlebar and down as far as the cable boss; leave enough slack to allow the handlebar to move freely when the cable is fitted and taped down. Cut the housing at the point where it reaches the cable boss – the resulting piece will be something like 50–60cm long. Use a sharp point to clear the opening at each end of the cable housing.

8

Place a ferrule over each end of the cable housing, then thread the gear cable through. Push the cable housing down so it slots into place in the shifters, then thread the cable carefully through the right-side cable boss and pull it taut. Verify that the cable won't impede handlebar movement, then thread the cable down and through the cable guide under the bottom bracket and along the chainstay.

Gear cables – housed all the way

On some bikes, mostly off-road models, the gear cable is housed all the way from shifter to derailleur. If this is the case, there won't be cable bosses but clips to hold the cable to the frame. Work out the length of housing you need by running a long piece from the shifter down to the derailleur. Cut the housing at the point where it reaches the rear derailleur's cable assembly – the resulting piece will be something like 190cm long. Use a sharp point to clear the opening at each end of the cable housing, pass the housing through the clips or guides on the frame, fit ferrules to each end, and pass the cable through it. Ensure that the housing slots into place in the shifters, fit it into the derailleur, pass the cable through, pull it taut and pass it through the cable-fixing bolt.

Brake cables

Unlike gear cables, brake cables don't arrive installed in the shifters, but fitting them is an easy job.

First, cut your cable housings to the correct length. Make sure that you take the (thicker) brake cable housing, not gear cable housing.

Front rim brakes

You need one piece of about 45cm to connect the right-hand shifter directly to the caliper mounted at the top of the fork.

Front disc brakes

You need one piece of about 80cm to connect the right-hand shifter directly to the caliper mounted at the bottom of the fork.

Rear rim brakes

The cable will probably be routed – exposed – along the top tube, with bosses at either end. In that case, you need one piece of cable housing (approximately 45cm) to connect the shifters to the cable stopper at the front of the top tube, and a second piece (approximately 22cm) to connect the rear cable stopper to the brake callipers. If there are no cable bosses, then the cable needs to be housed for its entire length – approximately 105cm for a medium-sized bike.

Rear disc brakes

The cable housing will probably run all the way from the shifters to the rear brake callipers – about 150cm. Your frame may have clips or other fittings which the cable housing will fit into – possibly secured by cable ties.

Count out the ferrules that you need for each end of the brake cables (2 for the front and either 2 or 4 for the rear brakes). Double-check that the brake cable itself is compatible with your shifters (Campagnolo has a slightly smaller head on the end of its cabling). Prepare four 10cm lengths of insulation tape. Fold up the base of each shifter's rubber hood.

Fitting the front brake cable (for caliper or disc brakes)

1

Start with the front (right-hand) brake Standing in front of the bike, depress the brake lever and look inside the mechanism. Inside, you will see a small housing with a hole: thread one end of the brake cable through it, and gently feed the cable in, taking care not to splay the ends. The cable will emerge at the base of the shifter. Gently take this end and pull it through until the brake lever is pulled into the open position. Double-check that the head of the cable is secure in its housing.

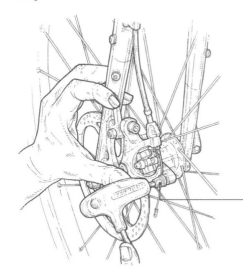

2

Now, take the front piece of cable housing: fit a ferrule over one end, then feed the brake cable into that end and pull it along until the cable housing beds down into the slot at the base of the shifters. Tape the cable housing to the handle bar to hold it in place. Pass the cable housing through any guides fitted to the fork.

3

Fit a ferrule to the other end of the cable housing by threading the cable through it. Then, carefully thread the cable through the barrel adjuster at the brake calliper and on through the cable clamp. When all the cable is pulled through, pull it taut and lock down the cable clamp with a hex key.

4

Double-check that the cable housing is securely bedded in at each end, that there is no slack in the cable and that the brake lever is held in the open position. Trim the cable about 10cm beyond the clamp and pinch a cable end into place with pliers.

Fitting the rear brake cable (rim or disc brake)

1

If your brake cable runs in its housing all the way to the rear brakes, then simply repeat the process on page 75, but running the cable in its housing from the left shifter through to the rear brake calliper, passing it through the cable guides on the frame as you do so.

2

If the cable runs exposed between two bosses on the top tube on its way to the rim brake, then take the shortest piece of cable housing, place ferrules on each end, and seat it in the rear cable stopper and the barrel adjuster. It will stay in place. Then repeat the above process, but running the cable in its housing from the left shifter through to the front cable stopper.

3

Thread the cable from there to the rear cable stopper and it will be guided through the barrel adjuster towards the cable clamp. Check tension, tighten into the clamp and trim as above.

Fitting cable ends to brake and gear cables

1

Lightly grip the cable end in the pincers of your pliers.

2

Slide it over the trimmed end of the cable.

3

And grip firmly so the cable end is squashed firmly in place.

2.15 Fitting the tyres

For many years, you either rode with high-end racing tyres, or you combined a pressurized inner tube with a tough outer 'clincher' tyre. Both systems had disadvantages: racing tyres are difficult to fit and have a limited life, while inner tubes are heavy and can't be run at low pressures. Both systems are vulnerable to punctures, the bane of the cyclist's life.

The advent of tubeless tyres in the early 2000s finally supplied an alternative solution – one that uses an outer tyre very similar to the traditional kind, combined with an airtight wheel rim and an ingenious latex solution that plugs punctures in the blink of an eye. Initially adopted by the mountain bike community, tubeless systems are now common on road and gravel bikes.

Fitting a new tyre and inner tube

1

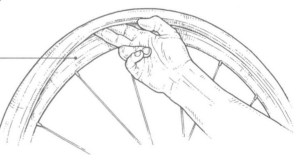

Take the tyre and fit one side over the rim of the wheel and into the gully in the centre. As a double-check, run your fingers around the inside of the tyre and the rim to make sure that no grit or foreign body has made its way in.

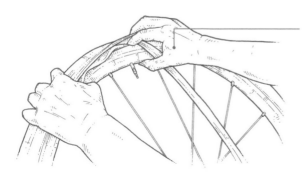

2

Take the inner tube and insert the valve through its hole, making sure the inner tube at that point is enclosed by the tyre. Work the inner tube into the tyre all the way round. Screw the locknut on to the valve, but don't tighten it down. Pump a little air into the tube so that it holds its shape but isn't stiff.

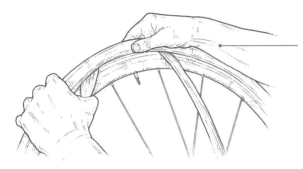

3

With your thumbs, and starting at the valve, start bedding the tyre into the wheel rim. Do this with both hands at the same time, face the wheel, making sure you don't pinch the inner tube between the tyre and the rim.

4

When you've done the first half, rotate the wheel and start working your hands towards each other until nearly all the tyre bead is bedded back into the rim.

5

A final stretch of about 15cm may be tricky. If it is, take a tyre lever and reach the point under the tyre bead so that it engages with the wheel rim, then push it up so that the bead snaps in. Wetting the rim with a little water may lubricate it.

6

Pump up the tyre, checking that the inner tube isn't pinched at any point.

Fitting a tubeless system

Double-check that your wheel rim and chosen tyres are both tubeless-compatible. If they aren't, it's back to inner tubes.

If the ends of the spokes go through the wheel rim, then you need to apply a layer of airtight tape to seal the gaps (many new wheels arrive with tape fitted already).

The tape needs to be 1–2mm wider than the base of the rim in which it will sit – refer to the table, right. (The rim bed width is the second number given in the wheel's specification – for instance, 700x25.) An easy way to double-check is to hold the roll of tape against the wheel rim beads. If the roll slots in, it's not wide enough. If it sits on top of the beads, then it is.

TAPE WIDTH	RIM BED WIDTH
22mm	Up to 17mm
24mm	18–21mm
27mm	22–25mm
32mm	26–30mm
36mm	31mm+

It's easier to apply the tape straight if the wheel is steady, so place it in the frame at a comfortable working height. Make sure your hands are clean.

The rim needs to be thoroughly cleaned and dried before you apply the tape – a quick way to do this without leaving residue is to use isopropyl alcohol (rubbing alcohol) and a clean rag.

1

Find the point on the rim directly opposite the hole for the valve. You start laying the tape here, near where the wheel's welded joint is. Start laying the tape about 10cm before the joint so it passes over it: hold the end of the tape firm as you pull it tight and stick about 20–30cm of tape down.

Rotating the wheel away from you, and pulling the tape tight, lay down another 20–30cm, repeating until you have made your way round the rim. When you have overlapped your starting point by about 10cm, cut the tape neatly with scissors and press the end down firmly.

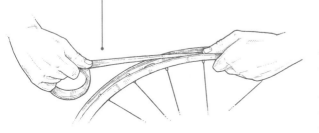

2

Take the cloth and wipe down the tape all the way round, cleaning it and also pressing it firmly onto the rim so there are no bubbles trapped underneath it. Do this three times: once down the centre channel and once down each bead seat.

3

Locate the valve hole. With a sharp point, prick into it through the rim tape, making a small hole. Take the tubeless valve, with the cap off and the top nut screwed down, and push it through the hole so that it pops out the other side. Fit the locknut to the thread and tighten it with your fingers to keep the valve firmly in place. Next, take the wheel off the bike.

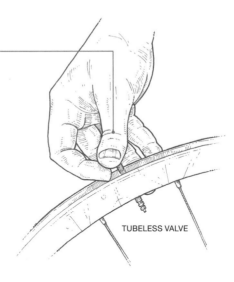

TUBELESS VALVE

4

Consult the bottle of your chosen sealant to find the right amount for your tyre size. Pour this into a kitchen measuring cup. Pour a few drops onto the fitted rim tape at the point where the valve is stuck through it to seal the hole.

Which sealant?

There are many latex solutions to choose from and they vary in price and effectiveness. A rigorous set of comparison tests conducted by the website road.cc found *Stan's No Tubes Race Sealant* and *Effetto Mariposa Caffélatex* to be the best performers.

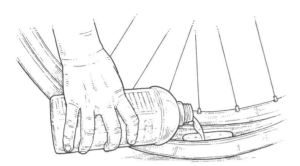

5

Now fit the tyre around the rim, fitting one side completely, but leaving an opening about 15cm long on the other. Hold the wheel vertically so the opening is at the bottom. Carefully pour the sealant into this opening, and then rotate the wheel 180 degrees so the opening is now at the top and the sealant can't spill out. Fit the last part of the tyre inside the rim, then rotate the whole wheel once to spread the latex and coat the inside of the tyre.

6

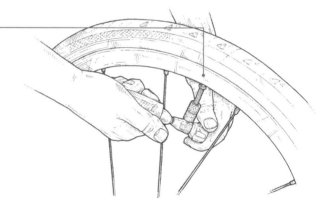

To form the initial latex seal, you need to fill the tyre very quickly; the easiest way to do this is using a CO_2 cartridge. Fit one into its inflator head without screwing it down, screw the head to the open tyre valve and then carefully screw the CO_2 cartridge down so the seal bursts. The tyre will fill instantly (making a series of loud pops – don't be alarmed) and the seal will form. Give the tyre a good shake (holding it horizontally) to spread the latex evenly around the interior. Turn over and shake it again. Repeat the process with your other tyre.

7

Note that CO_2 leaks from tyres much more quickly than either oxygen or nitrogen, so you will need to top up the gas in the tyres regularly using a hand pump over the next few days until all the CO_2 has seeped out and been replaced.

Working with latex

Latex is amazing stuff, but some people are allergic to it. If you are, fit tubeless tyres with extreme caution, or ask a friend to do the job for you – you will need to handle a lot of liquid latex solution, and small spills or even sprays are very likely, especially if it's your first time.

2.16 Tyre pressure

Nothing makes a more immediate difference to the quality of your ride than the pressure of your tyres. Everyone has their own preference, but whether you like a high- or a low-pressure ride, it's a real advantage to have a track pump with a pressure gauge to give you an objective readout when you're at home.

The safe pressure range for your tyres will always be written on their sides: use the table below, which should keep you safely within those parameters, to get the best pressure for you. Bear in mind the following factors:

- A heavier rider should use higher pressures; a lighter rider, lower. One easy way to take this into account is to add 1PSI in pressure for each 5kg you are over 70kg in weight, or subtract 1PSI in pressure for each 5kg you are under 70kg in weight. If you are riding on road tyres you can add or subtract more – up to 2PSI per 5kg.

- If you ride off-road, you will want a slightly softer tyre for better grip.

- If you want to go fast on-road you should increase the pressure.

- Tubeless tyres can run at lower pressures than the equivalent tubed tyre.

- Your rear tyre carries more of your weight, so a slightly higher pressure is more appropriate for it.

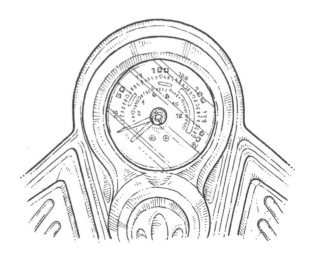

	TYRE WIDTH	FRONT TYRE PRESSURE	REAR TYRE PRESSURE
Mountain bike (tubeless)	45mm+	26PSI (1.8Bar)	28PSI (1.9Bar)
Mountain bike (with inner tube)	45mm+	36PSI (2.5Bar)	38PSI (2.6Bar)
Cyclocross/Gravel (tubeless)	37–43mm	36PSI (2.5Bar)	38PSI (2.6Bar)
Cyclocross/Gravel (with inner tube)	37–43mm	48PSI (3.3Bar)	50PSI (3.4Bar)
Hybrid (tubeless)	32–35mm	38PSI (2.6Bar)	40PSI (2.75Bar)
Hybrid (with inner tube)	32–35mm	50PSI (3.4Bar)	55PSI (3.8Bar)
Road bike (tubeless)	23–28mm	80PSI (5.5Bar)	83PSI (5.7Bar)
Road bike (with inner tube)	23–28mm	90PSI (6.2Bar)	93PSI (6.4Bar)

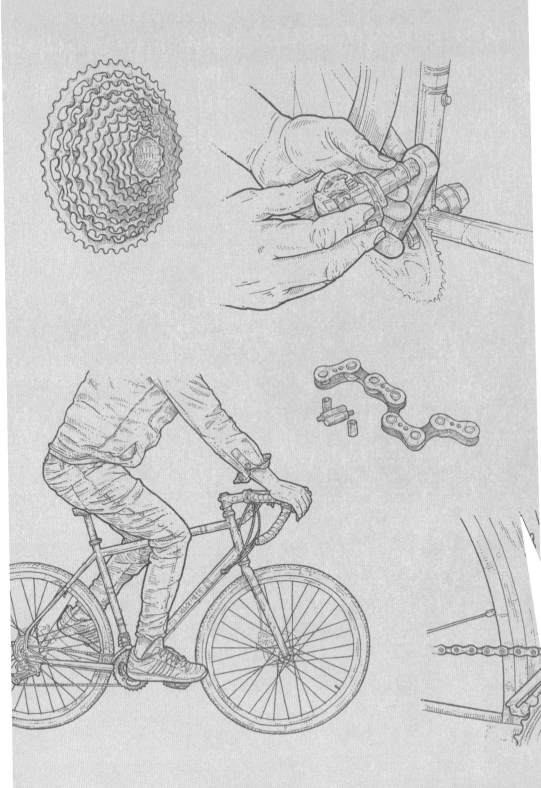

3
The Build
DAY TWO

Having laid down the foundations yesterday, today you'll fit the mechanical parts of the drive train – which converts the movement of your legs into rotations of the rear wheel – and get it moving in perfect harmony. The next step is to tune the brakes, after which you're ready for the first ride. This will tell you how everything's working, and let you troubleshoot and make fine adjustments to the ride position. Once that's done, all that remains is the handlebar tape!

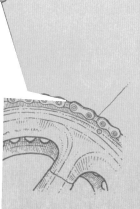

3.1 Fitting pedals

Now the crank is in, you can fit the pedals. It may seem obvious that right-side pedals need to go into the right-side crank and left-side pedals into the left side. Pro mechanics will, however, tell you that many people fail to realize this, and spend fruitless hours failing to attach pedals, sometimes even stripping the threads of the crank arm in the process. Don't make this mistake! All pedals, clipless or otherwise, will have a tell-tale R or L somewhere on them to help you: locate it and double-check before you fit.

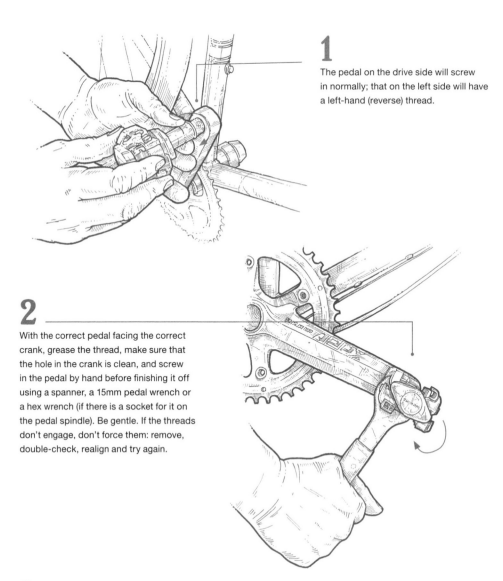

1
The pedal on the drive side will screw in normally; that on the left side will have a left-hand (reverse) thread.

2
With the correct pedal facing the correct crank, grease the thread, make sure that the hole in the crank is clean, and screw in the pedal by hand before finishing it off using a spanner, a 15mm pedal wrench or a hex wrench (if there is a socket for it on the pedal spindle). Be gentle. If the threads don't engage, don't force them: remove, double-check, realign and try again.

Adjusting a clipless pedal system

1

Both the positioning of the cleats on the shoe and the tightness of the pedal mechanism need to be properly adjusted for the pedals to be efficient, comfortable and safe. Fit the cleats so that they are under the ball of your foot and tighten using a hex key.

2

New pedals are usually supplied with the mechanism fully tightened; if you are unfamiliar with clipless systems, this makes it difficult to get your cleats in and out and you'll likely end up falling over when you come to a stop. Loosen both sides of each pedal using the hex bolts on the front and back, and practise clicking your feet in and out before using them for the first time on the road.

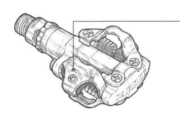

TIP: There are many clipless pedal and cleat systems out there, and (of course) only a few are mutually compatible. The illustrations here show Shimano's SPD system. This is affordable, tough and compatible with many shoes that can be comfortably worn off the bike.

3.2 Freehub and cassette

Re-directing all the power from your chain into the rear wheel, the junction of sprockets and hub is under great strain and has to be both robust and smooth-running. There are two basic patterns: the modern freehub-plus-cassette assembly, and the traditional (and inferior) threaded-hub-plus-freewheel assembly (see page 90).

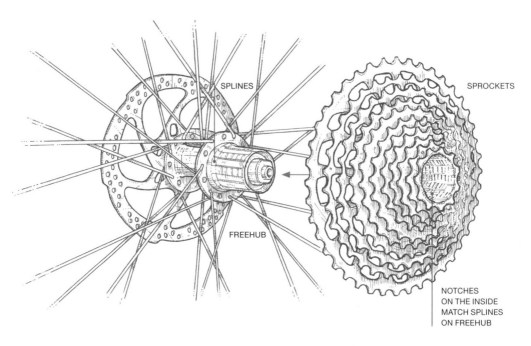

SPLINES

SPROCKETS

FREEHUB

NOTCHES
ON THE INSIDE
MATCH SPLINES
ON FREEHUB

Freehub plus cassette

Modern groupsets, including all 10-speed and 11-speed systems from the leading brands, use this system, in which the sprockets of the rear cassette slot over a splined (notched) cylindrical freehub that in turn is mounted on the wheel's hub. The splines match a pattern of indentations in the centre of each sprocket, and align the sprockets to make gear shifting smooth and quick. The freehub can spin freely anti-clockwise (allowing you to freewheel); when it rotates clockwise, sprung pawls (teeth) in its base engage with a circular ratchet in the wheel's hub, forcing the whole wheel to turn as one with the freehub.

Wheels and freehubs

When inspecting a new wheel, make sure that the freehub is tightly fitted, and that the wheel spins smoothly around it. That ticking sound you hear when freewheeling is healthy: it is the noise of the pawls inside the hub tapping against the gears of the ratchet.

Fitting the cassette

You will need a lockring tool – and note that Shimano and SRAM lockrings differ from Campagnolo.

Your cassette consists of a set of sprockets (one for each gear), most of which are single rings (although the lowest gears may be supplied as one unit), spacers that keep them apart and prevent the chain from fouling, and a lockring, which holds the whole assembly together. These have to be fitted in the right order. In order to make it easy to do so, most new cassettes come fitted to a plastic applicator: don't take the sprockets off this!

1

If you have an applicator, hold the wheel in your lap, hub side up, and very lightly grease the sides of the freehub. Hold the cassette on its applicator with both hands and rotate it until the pattern of splines on the applicator and freehub match, then ease the sprockets and spacers over the hub.

2

If you don't have an applicator, fit the sprockets and spacers one by one, making sure that they are in the correct order. The pattern at the centre of each sprocket needs to be aligned with the splines on the freehub.

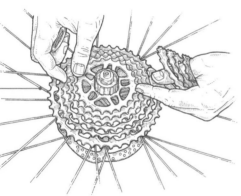

3

When all the sprockets and spacers are in place, screw on the lockring clockwise as tightly as you can with your fingers.

4

Insert the lockring tool and tighten it firmly using an adjustable-end wrench.

There should be no movement or wobble in the cassette: if there is, the freehub will swiftly be wrecked as you ride the bike – so make sure that it is firmly locked down.

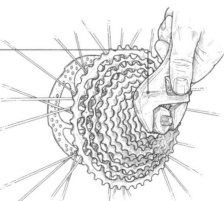

3.3 Freewheel

If you are restoring an old bike, or using second-hand or low-budget parts, you may come across an old-fashioned freewheel. These are easy to fit, but much harder to remove or maintain than modern freehub systems, and also put the axle and wheel bearings under more strain. They also offer a lower range of gears – typically between 5 and 8 – whereas freehubs can take 10 or more.

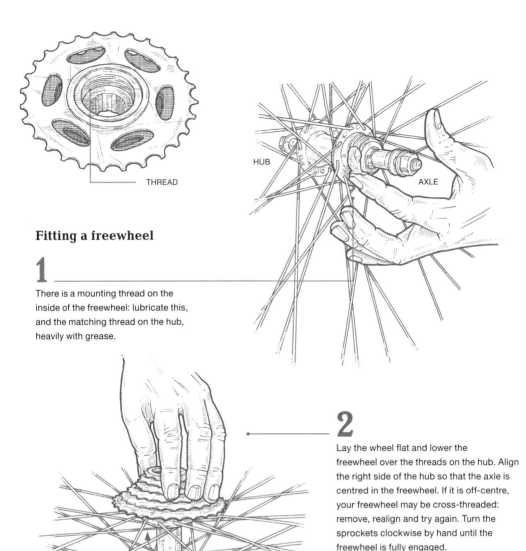

THREAD

HUB

AXLE

Fitting a freewheel

1

There is a mounting thread on the inside of the freewheel: lubricate this, and the matching thread on the hub, heavily with grease.

2

Lay the wheel flat and lower the freewheel over the threads on the hub. Align the right side of the hub so that the axle is centred in the freewheel. If it is off-centre, your freewheel may be cross-threaded: remove, realign and try again. Turn the sprockets clockwise by hand until the freewheel is fully engaged.

3

When the freewheel is engaged, tighten it up with the lockring tool – first by hand and then using a wrench to tighten it and seat the freewheel flush against the hub.

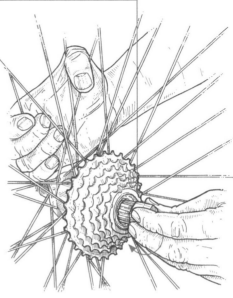

TIP: Fitting a freewheel is easier than taking it off again after thousands of kilometres of use, as the torque of riding screws it down. After a while, you will need a vice attached to a workbench – and, very possibly, a strong friend – to help you remove it, and the job often needs to be carried out by a pro with a workshop. This is another good reason to switch to a freehub.

3.4 Fitting the wheels

The brakes and gears can't be adjusted before the wheels are fitted, so now is the time to add them. Especially the first time, it is easiest to do this when the bike is upside down: flip the frame so it is resting on its saddle and handlebars.

Quick-release skewers

Most modern wheels are compatible with, and are often supplied with, quick-release skewers. These pass through the (hollow) axle. Although they don't carry any weight, they hold the axle (which does carry weight) securely in place in the dropouts, while allowing the wheels to be removed in a matter of seconds and without tools.

Front and back wheels are fitted in the same way. Remove the nut and one spring from the skewer and pass it through the wheel. The skewer can be fitted either way round. Replace the spring and give the nut a couple of turns with your fingers. Place the front wheel in the dropouts; the quick-release springs should be on the outside. You will see the axle come to rest on the dropouts and feel a satisfying clunk. If your wheel has disc rotors, adjust the callipers (which shouldn't be tightly attached to the frame at this point) so that the disc slides into its slot between them. Make sure that the lever is in the 'open' position, then turn the nut on the other end of the skewer clockwise until you feel resistance. Push the lever open to the 'closed' position (if it flips closed with no resistance, tighten the nut slightly). Repeat the process with the back wheel, taking care not to knock the rear derailleur.

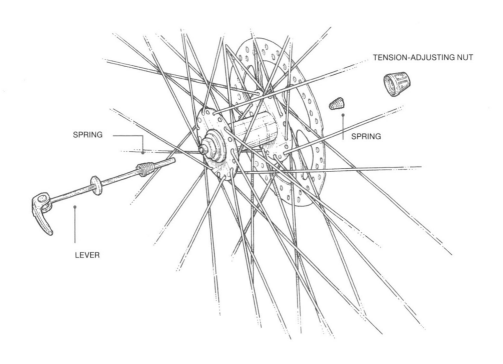

TENSION-ADJUSTING NUT

SPRING

SPRING

LEVER

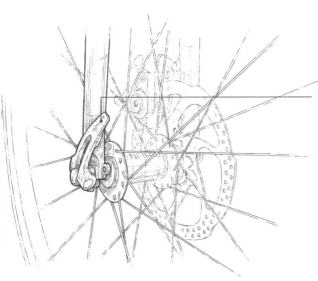

The lever will be easier to open if you close it so the handle is next to, but not directly in line with, the fork (front wheel) or seat stay (rear wheel); that way you can easily get your fingers round it and, if it is stiff, get purchase on the frame.

Spin the wheels to check that they are straight and in line with the frame, then flip the bike the right way up and put it back in the stand so that you can fit the chain and adjust the brakes.

3.5 Chain measuring and fitting

A chain that is too long or too short won't change properly and won't allow you to access the full range of gears, so it's essential to get the length right.

Chain length

There are a host of methods for ascertaining the correct length of chain, each with their own adherents (some using impressively complicated mathematical formulae), but this is one that I've used without problems.

Chains consist of 'open' or 'outer' links, and 'closed' or 'inner' links.

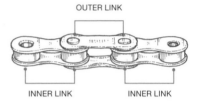

OUTER LINK

INNER LINK · INNER LINK

1

Marking the chain will make this job easier, so have a marker pen to hand. Place the bike on its stand high enough for you to work comfortably and sit facing the drive side. Make sure that you are familiar with how your power link (see page 40) works.

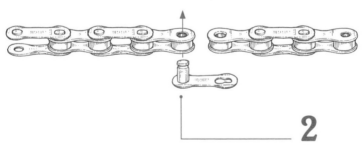

2

Place one half of the power link into an inner link at one end of the chain.

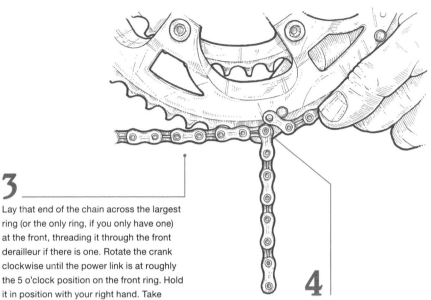

3

Lay that end of the chain across the largest ring (or the only ring, if you only have one) at the front, threading it through the front derailleur if there is one. Rotate the crank clockwise until the power link is at roughly the 5 o'clock position on the front ring. Hold it in position with your right hand. Take the other end of the chain and lay it over the largest sprocket on the rear cassette, making sure that the chain is fully engaged with the sprocket's teeth. That end will hang straight down.

4

Without passing it through the rear derailleur, pull the left end towards the power link in your right hand so the chain is taut. Find the first inner link that could connect to the power link and mark the rivet where they meet with the marker pen. That's your reference rivet.

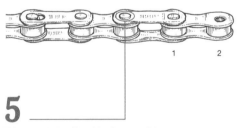

1   2

5

Take the chain off and lay it on a table. Count two rivets on from the reference rivet, then break the chain there so that an inner link is exposed at the end, ready to be connected to the power link.

NOTE: If you are using a SRAM 1x11 or 1x12 set-up (with a single front chainring, a long-cage derailleur and 11 or 12 sprockets on the cassette) and no suspension, then you should follow the above instructions up to Step 5, but break the chain four rivets on from the reference rivet.

Breaking a chain

Breaking a chain is easy and quick, but you *really* don't want to break a new chain in the wrong place, so always double-check that you have the right length before you do it. If necessary, repeat Steps 1–5 above to confirm that the link you have identified is in fact the correct one.

1

Seat the chain in your chain-breaking tool, with the correct rivet centred.

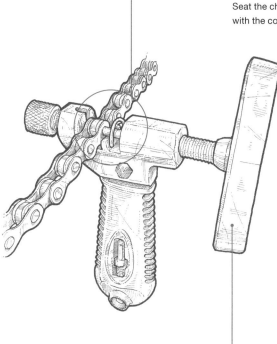

2

Turn the punch handle clockwise until it touches the head of the rivet. Check that its end rests in the centre of the rivet head, and that the other end of the rivet is not obstructed by the back of the tool.

3

Continue turning clockwise, driving the rivet out of the front plate and through the rear plate. It will pop out and the chain will divide.

NOTE: If you wish to return the chain to the bike (for instance, if you are removing it to service some other part), or if you need to add links to lengthen it, then do not push the rivet all the way through so it falls out. Instead, very slowly and carefully, drive it through until one end is still engaged in the outer plate, but the inner plates are both free. You can break the chain now and return the rivet to position using the same tool, pushing it back through from the other side of the chain.

Adding the power link and fitting the chain

With the shifters, adjust both front and rear derailleurs so they are aligned with the smallest sprockets, front and back. Run one end of the chain through the front derailleur. Don't engage it with the rings; just let it hang over the bottom bracket shell. Pass the other end over the smallest sprocket on the cassette, then feed it through the rear derailleur, making sure that it passes under the guides on the jockey wheel plate and engages with the jockey wheels (see page 70).

1

Take the ends of the chain and insert the two parts of the power link into the inner plates, one from each side of the chain so that they marry up. Carefully align the two halves of the power link, with the pins aligning with the wider end of the 'keyhole' in the other half.

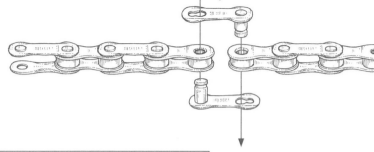

2

Squeeze the link together so the pins are seated in the holes.

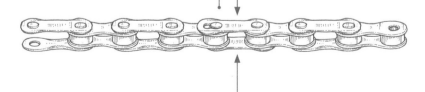

3

Then gently pull outwards so the pins slide along into the locked position.

Sometimes they connect, but don't slide outwards as far as they should to fully engage. If so, sit the chain around the largest ring on the crankset (you will need to adjust the front derailleur to do so)

and gently back-pedal so that the power link is carried up and round. Stop when it is halfway between the crank and the cassette. Hold the back wheel with your left hand; with your right hand, rotate the crank firmly clockwise – the power link will snap into place.

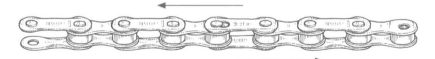

3.6 Adjusting the rear derailleur

With the chain fitted, you now need to adjust the derailleurs so that they move the chain smoothly from sprocket to sprocket and across the gears without jumping off.

Start with the rear mech. Set the stand so that you can easily look at the chain and derailleur from behind. First you'll set the high-limit screw, then you'll connect the gear cable and adjust its tension so that gear switching is precise, then you'll set the low-limit screw. You'll need a small cross-head screwdriver to set the limit screws.

1

Seat the chain on the small front ring (if you have two) or the middle (if you have three). Without any cable tension, the derailleur will naturally sit in a 'high' gear position. Rotate the cranks clockwise until the rear mech moves the chain onto the smallest sprocket. Stop!

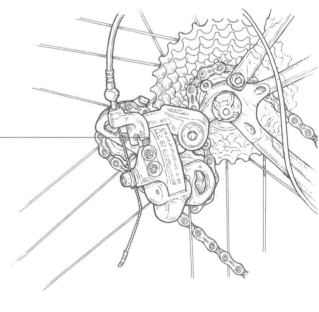

2

On the derailleur you will see the heads of a pair of screws. They will be marked with an H for high and an L for low. Identify the H screw, which governs the higher limit, or how far out towards the frame the derailleur can move. You want the derailleur to move out far enough for the chain to sit well on the smallest sprocket, but no further, as this will jam the chain between frame and cassette, bringing you to a stop without notice.

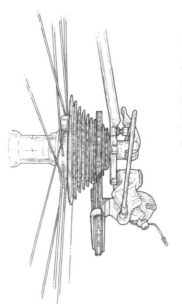

3

Turning the high-limit screw clockwise moves the jockey wheel inwards; anti-clockwise, outwards. With the screwdriver, adjust the screw so the uppermost jockey wheel is directly below the smallest of the sprockets.

4

Now you need to fit the cable. Loosen the cable anchor bolt with a hex key and sit the cable underneath it. Make sure that all the lengths of cable housing are seated firmly in their fittings on the frame. Turn the barrel adjuster on the derailleur clockwise until it stops, then turn it one turn anti-clockwise. If there is a barrel adjuster on the down tube, do the same there. On the shifter, select the highest gear (which translates into the lowest tension on the cable). At the other end, grip the cable (you can use a pair of pliers for this), pull it firmly taut and, without relaxing the cable, tighten the cable anchor bolt with the hex key.

Once it's tight, you can release the tension on the cable. Check the run of the cable again to make sure that it's snug in its fittings all the way up to the shifter.

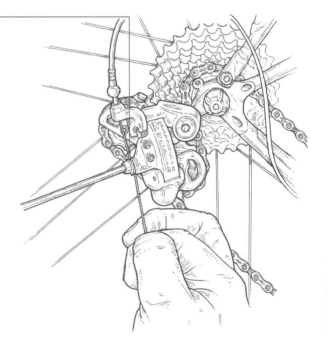

5

To tune the derailleur, turn the cranks gently forwards, moving up two gears on the shifter as you do so, so that the chain shifts into the third sprocket on the cassette. From behind the bike, look closely to see whether the jockey wheel is directly below the third sprocket (so that the chain runs perfectly vertically). If it isn't, use the barrel adjuster to fine-tune: turning it anti-clockwise increases the tension in the cable and shifts the derailleur inwards; turning it clockwise decreases the tension, shifting the derailleur outwards.

6

Once the jockey wheel is directly below the third sprocket, start turning the cranks slowly and shift up and down through the gears a few times, without going into the lowest gear. The mech should move one sprocket with each click of the shifter. If it is reluctant to move inwards onto larger sprockets, increase the cable tension with an anti-clockwise turn of the barrel adjuster. If it is slow to shift down to a smaller sprocket, or skips gears when you shift up, then loosen it with a clockwise turn.

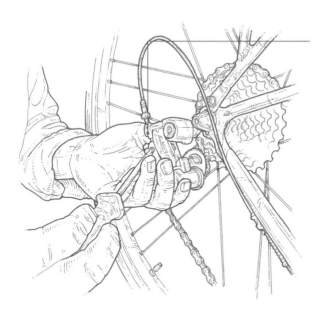

7

With the chain moving well over the sprockets, shift very carefully, one click at a time, onto the largest sprocket. Stop the wheel and locate the head of the screw marked L; this is usually sited just below the high-limit screw that you've already adjusted. This governs the lower limit, or how far inwards towards the spokes the derailleur can move. Now push the body of the derailleur inwards as far as it will go. The jockey wheel cage will probably move further inwards than the largest sprocket: you don't want this, as it will allow the chain to jump off the sprocket and get jammed in the spokes. Turn the L screw clockwise, and push the derailleur again to see where the limit now lies. Continue until the derailleur can go no further than the largest sprocket.

8

Test that this is working: turn the cranks slowly, and shift gears up and down around the large sprockets. When your chain is engaged on the largest sprocket, test the high limit by applying more tension to the cable with your shift lever. If you're alert, you'll see the chain starting to come off before it falls into the spokes. Quickly grab the wheel and rotate it backwards if that happens, then tighten the low-limit screw again.

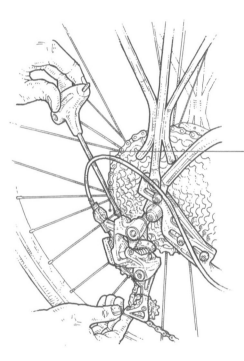

9

Finally, you need to adjust the body angle screw, or b-screw, if your derailleur has one (most, but not all, do). It is behind the mounting bolt at the back of the derailleur and determines how close the upper jockey wheel is to the cassette; it should be as close to the sprockets as possible, but not touching them. Turning the b-screw clockwise moves the jockey wheel away from the cassette; turning it anticlockwise, closer.

10

Adjust it until the gap is about 3–5mm. Give a final check to the shifting up and down of the gears, and adjust as necessary.
  With wirecutters, cut the cable about 2–3cm from the cable anchor bolt, and fit a cable end onto it before it can fray.

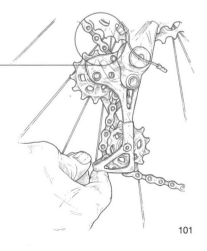

3.7 Adjusting the front derailleur

This is a much simpler mechanism than its rear sibling, but it needs tuning and adjustment too, to avoid rubbing and unpredictable shifting.

Double-check that the derailleur is at the right height on the seat tube, 2–3mm above the teeth of the largest chainring, and is parallel to the chainrings.

Front mechs work by pushing the chain from side to side so that its links catch on the teeth of the ring you want it to engage with. The two plates (the inner one, on the frame side, and the outer one, on the crank side) should not touch the chain when it is engaged on the ring.

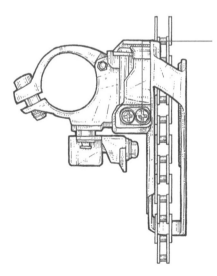

1

Put the chain on the smallest chainring. With no tension on the cable, the mech should be approximately in line with it. Just as with the rear mech, the front derailleur's travel is limited by two screws, which you should see on top of it: they may be identified by an L and an H. The nearer one to the frame usually controls the lower limit – how close to the frame the derailleur can move.

Adjust it so the inner plate sits just clear of the chain, and turn the crank a few times to make sure that there's no contact. If that screw doesn't move the derailleur, try the other one.

2

Now you need to fit the cable and its tension. Turn the barrel adjuster on the derailleur clockwise until it stops, then turn it one turn anti-clockwise. If there is a barrel adjuster on the down tube, do the same there. The cable will be routed underneath the bottom bracket and pop up to fit into the cable anchor bolt from below. Grip the cable, pull it firmly taut and, without relaxing the cable, tighten the cable anchor bolt with the hex key.

3

Now slowly turn the cranks so the chain is moving through the derailleur. Push the shift lever inwards to move the derailleur out onto the larger chainring. If the chain doesn't engage with the larger ring, turn the barrel adjuster anti-clockwise to increase the tension, and try again. If the mech refuses to move out as far as the big ring, try turning the upper limit adjuster screw to give the mech more travel.

4

Once the chain can engage with the big ring, turn the upper limit adjuster screw so the outer cage of the mech is 1–2mm clear of the chain. Give a final check to the shifting up and down of the gears, and adjust as necessary.

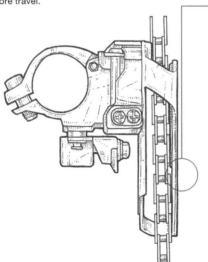

5

With wirecutters, cut the cable about 2–3cm from the cable anchor bolt and fit a cable end onto it before it can fray.

3.8 Tuning the brakes

You're nearly there! Your drive train is working smoothly, and you can move up and down through the gears, which will get you moving. Your next task is to tune the brakes so that you can stop.

Tuning disc brakes

Front and rear disc brakes are tuned in the same way. At this point, your brake callipers are already loosely bolted on to the frame or fork, allowing a certain amount of movement while you fitted the wheel.

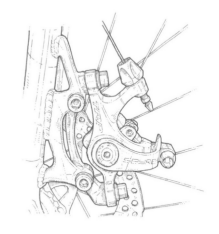

1

Pass the brake cable through its guide and bed the cable housing and ferrule into the barrel adjuster. Turn the barrel adjuster clockwise as far as it will go, then make one turn anti-clockwise.

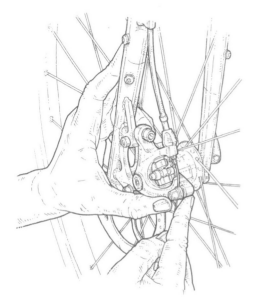

2

Pass the cable under its locking bolt and, gripping the end with pliers, pull it taut. Then tighten the locking bolt. With wirecutters, cut the cable about 2–3cm from the bolt and fit a cable end onto it before it can fray.

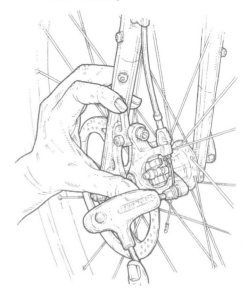

3

Now pull firmly on the brake lever: the brake pads should grip the rotors, and the callipers will shift on their loose mounting bolts accordingly. While holding them closed, tighten the mounting bolts with a hex wrench.

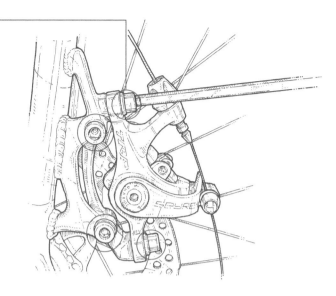

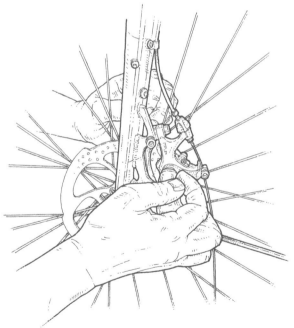

4

Spin the wheel to check that it's not catching on the rotors, and pull on the brakes firmly to verify that there is enough force: the callipers should firmly grip the rotors while the levers are still 2–3cm from the handlebars. If they need to be tighter, turn the barrel adjuster anti-clockwise. Some models also have a calliper adjuster on the side of the unit that you can tighten with a hex key.

Tuning calliper rim brakes

Front and rear brakes are tuned in the same way. At this point, your brake callipers are bolted on to the frame or fork, fully open as you fitted the wheel. If your brakes have a release lever to allow you to remove the wheel easily, set it to the closed position.

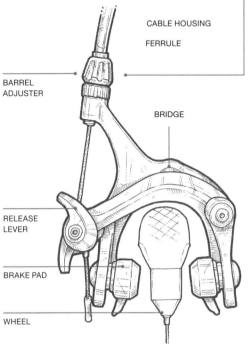

CABLE HOUSING

FERRULE

BARREL
ADJUSTER

BRIDGE

RELEASE
LEVER

BRAKE PAD

WHEEL

1

Turn the barrel adjuster clockwise as far as it will go, then two turns anti-clockwise. Bed the cable housing and ferrule into the barrel adjuster, and fit the cable into the clamp, passing the end through the pinch plates. There may be a groove in the inner faces of the plates that stops the cable getting squashed; this is where it sits. Tighten the bolt slightly so that the cable is held in place but is not locked down. Check that there is no play in the brake lever: if there is, pull more cable through from the brake end.

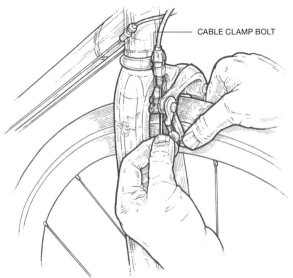

CABLE CLAMP BOLT

2

Grip the arms of the brakes and squeeze the blocks firmly against the rim. Pull at the end of the cable so that more of it passes through the cable bolt, then tighten it fully using a hex key while still holding the brakes closed. With wirecutters, cut the cable about 2–3cm from the bolt and fit a cable end onto it before it can fray.

3

Test the brakes by spinning the wheel and pulling on the levers: the callipers should firmly grip the rims while the levers are still 2–3cm from the handlebars. If they need to be tighter, turn the barrel adjuster anti-clockwise: if looser, turn the barrel adjuster clockwise.

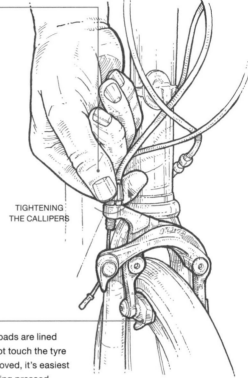

TIGHTENING
THE CALLIPERS

4

Make sure that the brake pads are lined up with the rims and do not touch the tyre itself: if they need to be moved, it's easiest to do so when they are being pressed gently against the wheel. With a piece of string or a strong rubber band, put pressure on the levers – enough to hold the blocks against the wheel, but not so much that you can't move them. With a hex key, loosen the bolt that holds them to the callipers and move them until they are well located. Tighten the bolt again, taking care not to twist the blocks as you do so.

3.9 Finding the perfect fit

Your position on the bike — governed by the relative positions of saddle, pedals and handlebars — is a matter of personal preference, but it is important to get the height of your saddle right: it dramatically affects how comfortable, effective and pain-free your pedalling is.

The three most important elements of the bike's fit are the saddle's height from the cranks (not from the ground); the distance from the saddle to the handlebars; and the height of the handlebars. Assuming you sized your frame correctly, it will be fairly simple to move the saddle, seatpost and bars relative to each other so that you have a comfortable ride and can spend a day in the saddle without discomfort.

Saddle height

Positioned next to a wall for balance, sit on the saddle, place your heel (not the ball of your foot) on the pedal and spin backwards to reach the lowest position. You are aiming for your knee to be completely straight: if it's still bent, raise the saddle by a small amount. If your heel loses contact with the pedal then you should lower the saddle. Make sure that you are not leaning to one side or the other, as this may lead to the saddle being too high. When you place the ball of your foot on the pedal in a riding position (pictured) your knee will be slightly bent.

Your kneecap should be just ahead of the pedal spindle.

Saddle position

Once the saddle is at the right height, you need to adjust it forward-to-back so that you are in a comfortable position relative to the pedals. A good guideline is known as KOPS: Knee Over Pedal Spindle. In this position, when the crank arm is level and pointing forward, your knee is directly above the spindle at the centre of your pedal. Put your feet in a riding position – the ball of your foot either directly over the spindle or very slightly (1cm) in front

of it: clip in, if that's how you ride. Set the crank at 3 o'clock, and dangle a metre rule (or any similar long straight object – I use the wheel-stabilizing rod from a bike stand) next to the front of your kneecap. As pictured above, it should be just in front of the pedal spindle. If it isn't, loosen the bolt (or bolts) on the base of the saddle and work it back or forwards along its rails until you are sitting in the right position.

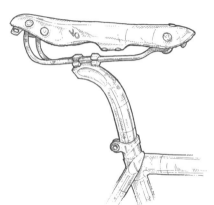

Saddle angle

The angle of your saddle is one area where a tiny adjustment can make a huge difference to your comfort, and it's something you should experiment with. Start with it level, then try tilting it slightly forward and back until you've found the most comfortable angle for you.

Bars and stem

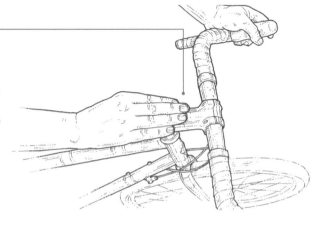

Reach is a much more subjective measurement than saddle height: there is no 'perfect' position. A good way to get yourself into the right ballpark is to stand by the bike, touch your elbow to the nose of the saddle and reach your hands towards the bars. The bars should be about three to four finger-widths past the tip of your fingers. It's easy to switch out the stem for a longer or shorter model if you want a more compact or more extended riding position. With drop bars, you will find that moving the shifters up or down can make a big difference to position and comfort. It is easy to do this before you put bar tape on, so now is the best time to experiment.

Handlebar height

Again, this is a matter of taste: a good starting point is to have your bars at about the same height as your saddle and raise or drop them depending on how upright or how aerodynamic you wish to be. A quill stem's height is easy to adjust using the bolt on top.

A threadless system is more difficult (and the range of possible heights is smaller, especially when the stem is cut), so avoid making a decision on cutting the stem until you are confident you have found the height you want to stick with. Try starting with no spacers under the stem, and adding them until you are comfortable.

3.10 First ride

It's the moment you've been looking forward to: although it's not quite finished, your new bike is ready to ride. Time to give it a test run to make sure that everything is as it should be.

Tuning rim brakes

However carefully you fitted these, it is likely that you will need to tune them to make sure that they deliver the right amount of stopping power. On a clear road, speed up and stop a few times using just the front brake. If you hear or feel the brake rubbing on the rim when you haven't pressed on the lever, you need to loosen it: turn the barrel adjuster half a turn clockwise, and then try again. If the wheel can still rotate when your brake lever is completely depressed, you need to tighten up: turn the barrel adjuster half a turn anti-clockwise, and try again. When your front brake is in good order, repeat the exercise with the rear brake.

Bedding in disc brakes

You need to bed in disc brakes, wearing them slightly so that the maximum area of the pad is pressed into contact with the discs. To do so, speed up to about 15km/h, then apply both brakes firmly and bring yourself down to about 5km/h (walking pace) without stopping, or locking the brakes. Repeat this about twenty times. Then speed up to about 30km/h (or as fast as you usually ride) and, again, brake yourself down to walking pace. Repeat this ten times.

Gears

Your gears should be fully functional right away, but it's worth running up and down the range a few times to make sure that they behave properly under load. Look out for persistently slow changes or skipped gears – these can be a sign that you need to realign the relevant derailleur slightly.

3.11 Handlebar tape

Once you've adjusted the fit, tuned the gears and brakes, and verified that everything's running smoothly, it's time to apply the finishing touch: an evenly applied roll of handlebar tape winding hypnotically around the bars.

Unlike most bike jobs, there is a definite knack to winding bar tape neatly. It is easy to get wrong, and as you spend plenty of time looking at the bars, small imperfections are disproportionately irritating. Follow these instructions, and don't be afraid to unwind and start again if you're going awry.

Bar tape varies in price, but the basic pattern is always the same: you have a long piece of padded plastic, cork or leather, usually with double-sided sticky tape running down the middle of one side. (Some brands don't have this, relying solely on elastic tension for their grip on the bars.) The sticky tape holds the bar tape onto your handlebars, but not very strongly: what keeps the bar tape in place is the tension you apply as you wind it on. Pulled slightly taut, wound in the correct direction, and firmly anchored at each end, bar tape should stay in place for many long rides.

A packet of bar tape normally holds two long rolls and two shorter pieces of padded tape, two plugs and two short pieces of a more strongly adhesive, finishing tape. You will need all of these and a pair of scissors. If your brake and gear cables are routed to run along the bars, you will also need four 10cm lengths of electrical tape.

1

First, clean and dry the bars to maximize the tape's adhesion to them. Place the bike in your stand with the bars at a comfortable working height and secure the front wheel with the stabilizer: it is much easier to wind tape if you don't have to bend down or worry about the bars wobbling.

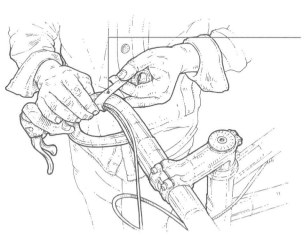

2

Using two pieces of electrical tape, pin the gear and brake cables down snugly into the corner of the bars, and bed them into the groove (if there is one) on the front of the bars. On each side of the bars, loop another piece at the point where you want the bar tape to end (normally about 5–6cm from the edge of the stem) – this will be your marker later on. Make sure that these pieces are symmetrically applied. Finally, fold up the hoods of the shifters so that you can apply tape neatly around their bases.

3

Now take one of the long pieces, pull back the cover of the adhesive tape on the inside and wind the tape around the open (bottom) end of the handlebar so that half the thickness of the tape extends off the end. It is important to roll the tape outwards over the top of the handlebar tube: this ensures that the torque of your grip on the bars is in the same direction as the tension that you put into the tape as you wind it. The tape needs to be tense, but don't stretch it too hard or it may snap. Wind the tape around the bar, making sure that the tape overlaps itself by about a third of its width. Use the adhesive strip down the middle as a guide: it should be on the bar, not the layer of tape below. This will ensure that you have an even wind. As you come to the curves, take extra care to make sure that you overlap the previous wind and that you maintain the tension.

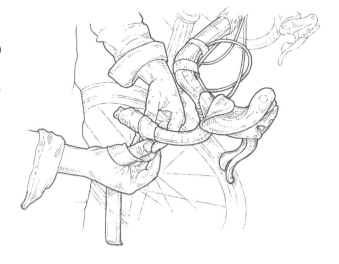

4

Carry on winding evenly until you meet the bottom of the shifter. At its base, direct the tape out, up and then back in over the top.

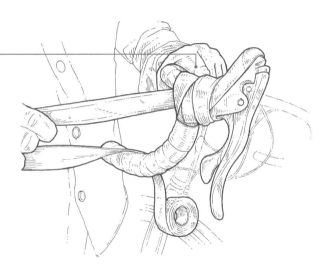

5

Wind once round underneath the shifter again, out and back in over the top of the bars again.

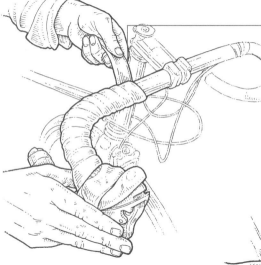

6

Continue winding along the top of the bars; the tape should run forwards over the top of the bar. Continue until you have reached the point where you want the tape to end.

7

In order to make a clean edge at the point where the last turn of tape folds over itself, you'll need to snip the end with scissors so it forms a point. Cut in from the leading edge of the tape, about 10cm, as shown.

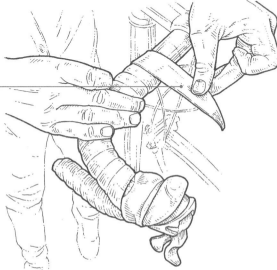

8

When that is done and the edge lines up neatly, take the finishing tape and stick one end onto the tapered end of the bar tape so that about half of it overlaps. Pull it taut, then wind it squarely round the bar so that it lies over itself, pulls the end of the bar tape tight and binds everything to the bars.

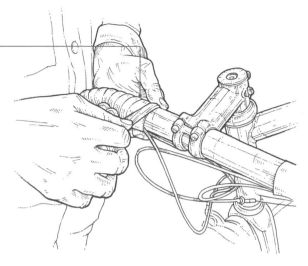

9

Now go back to the beginning, where your first turn around the bottom of the drops will still be open.

10

Fold the tape into the tube and press the bar end in after it to secure. Some bar ends have a screw that holds them more firmly in place. If yours does, tighten it now with a hex key.

11

Repeat the process on the other side of the bars.

Congratulations! You've just finished your bike. You can now put this book down and enjoy the ride.

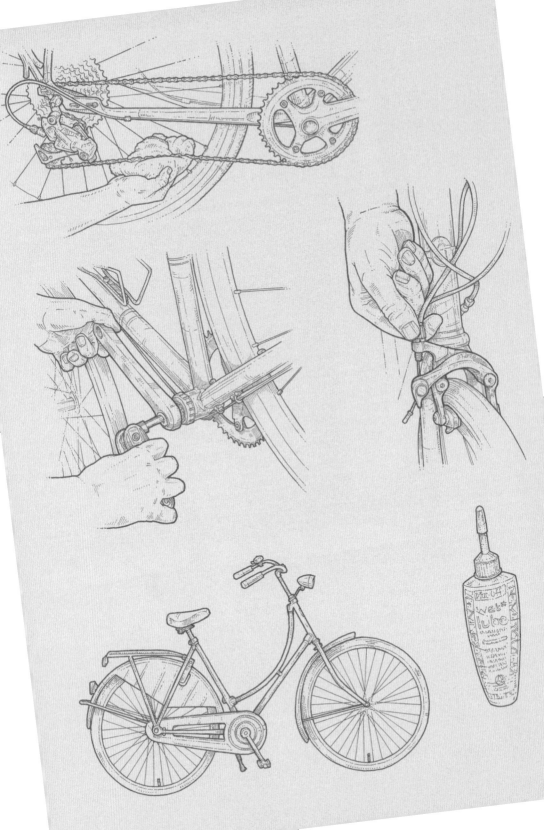

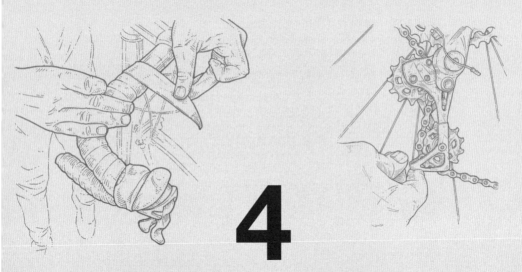

4
Maintenance

If you ride a bike, you have to look after it. Some
components wear out, others need to be lubricated to
stay healthy, and dirt from your rides builds up and
eventually causes problems. The good news is that a
little maintenance goes a long way – it only takes a
few moments to check your tyres and lubricate your
chain – and keeps you moving smoothly,
without risk of breakdown.

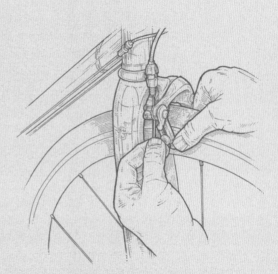

4.1 Regular checks

A few minutes of care from time to time will keep your new machine looking good, sounding healthy and running smoothly. You will stop most problems before they get serious or expensive, and your bike will reward you with a better ride.

Annual service

By removing only a few components, checking, cleaning and regreasing them, you can keep your bike humming year after year. By doing so you will also reduce the risk of corrosion – and of components getting permanently stuck in place – which is a nightmare when you need to replace or upgrade a part.

Pedals

Subject to continuous force and the very worst of bad weather and terrain, pedals are susceptible to getting stuck in their cranks so that high levels of force and a long-armed wrench are needed for removal. Removing them completely once a year, cleaning and regreasing the threads before replacement, will help.

Seatpost

Metal seatposts are prone to corrosion, which can lodge them permanently in your frame's seat tube. Avoid this by removing the post once a year, cleaning and regreasing it and the seat tube, and replacing.

Bottom bracket

Water can collect inside a frame at the bottom bracket, causing corrosion. Once a year, it is worth checking that everything is okay: remove the crankset, unscrew the bottom bracket, clean inside the shell, clean the bottom bracket threads, regrease and replace.

Tyres

You should check your tyres before every ride: when pumping them up, give the sides of your tyres a quick check for fraying, and the rolling surface a quick check for bald spots.

Rim brakes

Over time you'll notice your brakes becoming weaker as the pads wear out. You can maximize the life of your pads by slightly tightening the brake callipers to compensate: rotate the barrel adjuster once anti-clockwise, check and, if necessary, give it a further rotation. Once you've done this a couple of times, it is worth checking the pads. If the surface has been worn smooth and there are no longer any grooves in the surface of the pad, they should be replaced. When you replace the pads you should return the barrel adjuster to its starting position.

Disc brakes

The brake pads on disc brakes wear out, too, and will lose power over time. You can tighten the brake callipers to compensate: turn the barrel adjuster once anti-clockwise, check and, if necessary, turn once again. Once you've done this a couple of times, you should remove the wheel and check the pads visually. If you have less than a couple of millimetres of pad material on the metal backing plate, it's time to replace them.

A happy healthy chain

This part of the bike – always under strain, completely exposed to the elements, perfectly placed to capture dirt, dust and mud thrown up from the road, and pushed abruptly round by derailleurs – takes more punishment than any other, and needs more TLC than any other part of your bike.

Regular chain care

The most important thing is to keep your chain well lubricated and clean. The best time to look after it is just after a ride: this ensures that water and road crud doesn't have time to start corroding the chain's links, and it gives your chain lube time to penetrate the chain's interior before the next ride.

Lightly apply a drop of lube to the top of each link and then smear it into the cracks by running the tips of finger and thumb lightly along the chain. Take a rag and use it to clean off the sides of the chain – the lube is needed on the inside of the chain, not the outside. That's it.

If you're commuting, then a daily clean isn't necessary, but try to check your chain weekly, and definitely refresh the lube after you've ridden in the rain.

If you don't look after a chain, it will start to complain, rusting up and becoming stiff and noisy. Show it some love, as soon as you can, and you'll quickly notice an improvement in its behaviour.

When to replace the chain

All chains stretch slightly over time, and when they get too long they stop working properly, jumping from cog to cog and not engaging properly with the teeth on your chainring or cassette. There is no hard and fast rule as to how many kilometres you can expect from a chain. A lot depends on the way you ride, how much you weigh, and how well you look after it, but once the chain wear is 0.75 percent and 1.0 percent (i.e., when it has been stretched that much in use) it is time for a change. Quickly check it using a chain wear tool from time to time.

Rest the tool on a link on your chain: if the 0.75 percent point fits into a gap between the links, your chain will soon need replacing. If the 1.0 percent side fits in, do it now.

If you don't measure and replace your chain in good time you will find that it starts misbehaving, especially when under a heavy load. You will experience slow, unpredictable gear changes, and the chain may spontaneously jump from one gear to another. If it gets this bad, you should replace the cassette at the same time, as a badly worn-out chain will have worn out the sprockets on the cassette.

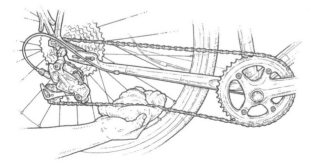

Cleaning a very dirty chain

If you've spent a day off-road, you will probably need to clean more thoroughly before applying the lube. You can do this with a wet rag, a stiff brush, or a chain-cleaning device. In any case, use a citrus-based solvent in warm water to lift the dirt off: let the chain dry, and then apply lube as above. Don't let a chain remain damp and unlubricated – it will start to rust up in days.

4.2 Truing a wheel

Spoked bicycle wheels are one of the engineering marvels of the world, but they take quite a beating, and need to be true to roll properly. A small kink can usually be minimized or removed with careful adjustment of spoke tension.

If you have rim brakes, you'll know when a wheel has a kink because it will start rhythmically hitting the brake pads: true it as soon as you can. If you have disc brakes, inspect your wheels regularly by flipping the bike upside down, spinning a wheel, observing it from directly in line and noting any 'wobble'. If you do spot a kink or wobble in your rim, don't delay – fix it before it gets any worse. If a wheel is bent to the point that you can't ride on it any more, it may well be fixable, but might be a job for a trained pro.

The secret to successfully truing a wheel is to be careful and methodical. It is easy to make the problem worse by rushing it, so never attempt to true a wheel if you're in a hurry; make yourself comfortable before you start and take your time.

The shape of the wheel depends on the tension in its spokes, and you will need to adjust that tension by tightening or loosening spokes at the point where they meet the rim.

Broken spokes need replacing before you can ride on the wheel again. There are several different patterns of spoke design and many different hubs, and there isn't the space to cover the subject properly here. Refer to the manufacturer's manual and website if you want to tackle this yourself.

1

Place the bike in the stand, and seat yourself in line with the wheel that needs fixing at eye height. First, you need to identify any loose spokes. Pluck all of the spokes on the wheel to make sure that they are tensioned and give you a similar note when plucked. If one is loose, tighten it with anti-clockwise turns of the spoke wrench until it feels approximately as tense as the other spokes (and makes a similar tone when plucked).

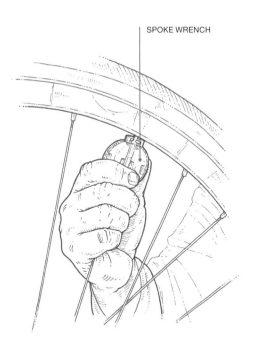

SPOKE WRENCH

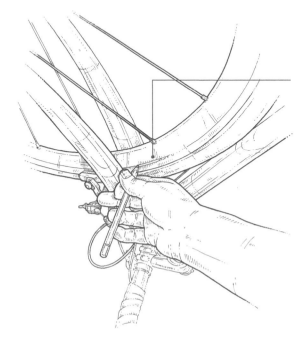

2

Now you need to locate exactly where the problem is. Spin the wheel and note which side the kink protrudes. Hold a pencil firmly braced against a brake pad, stay or fork so that the point of it is close to, but not touching, the wheel rim on that side. Spin the wheel; as it turns slowly, move the pencil towards the rotating rim. Its point will touch at the point where the wheel bulges and leave a line that shows you exactly which spokes need adjusting.

3

Now move so that you are facing the line. The spoke nearest to the mark will need the most adjustment. You must first identify if this spoke meets the hub on the near or far side of the wheel. Refer to the instructions below and apply them to the appropriate diagram for the adjustment you need to make.

Adjusting when the spoke meets the far side

If the spoke meets the hub on the far side of the wheel, loosen the two spokes on either side of it, then tighten it.

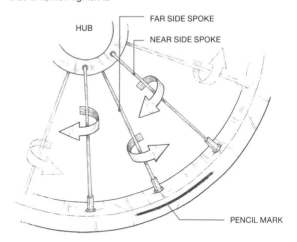

HUB

FAR SIDE SPOKE

NEAR SIDE SPOKE

PENCIL MARK

Adjusting spokes

• Loosen a spoke by turning the tool a half-turn clockwise.

• Tighten by turning the tool a quarter-turn anti-clockwise.

• Tightening the spokes that connect the rim to the far side of the hub will pull the rim away from you. Loosening the same spokes will bring the wheel towards you.

• Tightening the spokes that connect the rim to the near side of the hub will pull the rim towards you. Loosening the same spokes will pull the rim away from you.

Bearing these principles in mind, use the spoke tool to loosen and tighten the spokes nearest the kink by about half a turn each, as appropriate. Spin the wheel to see how much it has helped. If necessary, repeat and continue until the wheel is true again. Check frequently and don't be afraid to reverse a turn you've made.

Adjusting when the spoke meets the near side

If the spoke meets the hub on the near side of the wheel, loosen it, then tighten the two spokes on either side of it.

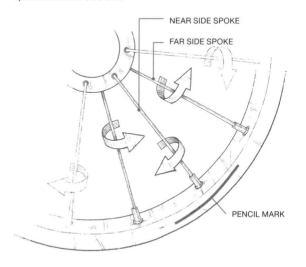

NEAR SIDE SPOKE

FAR SIDE SPOKE

PENCIL MARK

Checklists

Use these lists to ensure that you source all the parts you need, and that they will work together. Note that, where part compatibility is an issue, it may be highlighted more than once, as a double-check. Most of the information you need will be found on manufacturer's websites; space is given here for you to record the key numbers, for ease of cross reference. If you are restoring an old bike, then the late Sheldon Brown's website (sheldonbrown.com) has huge amounts of information about vintage frames and components.

FRAME + FORK CHECKLIST

COMPONENT	NOTE	CONSIDERATIONS
Frame Make and Model		
Material		
Size		
Geometry	Head tube: _____ Seat tube: _____	
Fork		Check the steerer tube diameter and whether it's threaded
Maximum tyre clearance		
Rim or disc brake fittings?		
If disc brake, what size rotors?	Front: _____ mm Rear: _____ mm	
If disc brake, flat mount or post mount?		
Pannier and mudguard fittings?		
Front derailleur: band-on or braze-on fitting?		If band-on, what seat tube diameter clamp?
Axle spacing: front		Usually 100mm
Axle spacing: rear		Usually 130mm (rim brake) or 135mm (disc): double-check
Bottom bracket shell		
Dropouts		
Seat tube	_____ diameter	
Headset fitted or included?		
Fork crown race fitted or included?		
Headset size, if not fitted	_____ diameter	
Headset bearings x 2		

GROUPSET CHECKLIST

COMPONENT	NOTE	CONSIDERATIONS
Bottom bracket		Check width, frame compatibility and crankset/ spindle compatibility
Crank: length	_____ mm	
Crankset – 1,2,3 wheel?		If installing a 3-ring crankset, check that the frame, front derailleur and rear cassette are compatible
Front derailleur: band-on or braze-on?		Will be determined by choice of frame. If band-on, check seat tube diameter
Shifters		Confirm compatibility with the rear derailleur
Rear derailleur		Confirm compatibility with the shifter and cassette
Cassette		Confirm compatibility with the rear derailleur and freehub
Chain		Confirm compatibility with cassette; if the frame is XL, have two to hand
Brakes: rim		Check fit with tyres (ensure callipers will clear tyres)
Brakes: disc		Check whether post-fit or flat-mounted, and that adapters are included if necessary
Brake Rotor Diameter		Check diameter against frame and fork spec
Cables: brake		
Cables: gear		
Cables housings: brake		
Cables housings: gear		
Ferrules		
Cable ends		

WHEEL CHECKLIST

COMPONENT	NOTE	CONSIDERATIONS
Size		Usually 770C, possibly 650B, or the mountain bike equivalent in each case
Tubeless or clincher?		
Construction		Confirm that the spoke count, hub and rim material are suitable for intended use
Freehub (or freewheel) included?		
Freehub compatibility		Shimano/SRAM or Campagnolo?
Braking compatibility		Rim or disc?
Axle spacing: front		Check that matches frame, above
Axle spacing: rear		Check that matches frame, above
Tyres: sizing		Check that size is correct, and that tyre width is compatible with the rim width, frame and forks
Tyres: inner tube or tubeless		Check that rim is compatible with tubeless systems if desired
Skewers		Check compatibility with hub and frame dropouts

OTHER COMPONENTS

COMPONENT	NOTE	CONSIDERATIONS
Handlebars	_____ mm diameter	Check that diameter is compatible with stem
Handlebar tape or grips		
Stem (quill or separate)		
Stem: handlebar compatibility	_____ mm diameter	
Stem: length		
Seatpost	_____ mm diameter	Check diameter against the seat tube
Pedals		If using clipless pedals, check that they are compatible with the shoes you will wear
Saddle		

SUPPLIES

Grease		
Chain lube		
Pump		
CO_2 cartridges		
Latex for tubeless tyres		

Further reading and reference

I have a few books about bicycle maintenance. Of them, *Zinn and the Art of Road Bike Maintenance* is the one that bears the most greasy thumbprints, so that's the one I recommend. Written by Lennard Zinn, it's the best (and biggest) current single-volume guide to looking after your bike.

The internet is stuffed with fascinating and informative resources for the cycle mechanic, and, while writing this book, I checked in with more websites, blogs and forums than it is possible to list here. That said, the YouTube channels of Park Tool and Global Cycling Network were particularly useful and are strongly recommended.

Index

Acknowledgements

Thanks firstly to Al Bailey, who modelled for the illustrations and generously shared his professional expertise. I'm also grateful to the rest of the people at Cranks, a not-for-profit bicycle cooperative in Brighton: in particular Iain, Dave and Adam. If you are lucky enough to have a place like that in your home town, support it. You can learn about their work at cranks.org.uk.

I'm hugely grateful to the people who made this book happen. Zara Larcombe commissioned it. Chelsea Edwards steered it to completion, calmly working around some quite appalling tardiness from the author. Alex Coco took pains to make every spread not only clear but elegant, and it was a real privilege to work with Lee John Phillips for the first, and I hope not the last, time. Felicity Awdry looked after the book's production. Sid Allen took the last crucial reference photos. It goes without saying that any errors that made it through are mine. As ever, many thanks to the rest of the brilliant team at Laurence King Publishing – including Barney, Fiona, Marc, Laurence, Adrian, Angus, Felicity, Myrsini, and the people of Chronicle Books and LKP Verlag.

Authors are known to do obnoxious things in the cause of their art, and I contributed to that long, ignoble tradition by parking the contents of a bike workshop in the bathroom for several months. LB de la Mer and Sid Allen never once complained about this incredibly inconsiderate behaviour. Neither did Jules Hau: for that, and much more than I could ever express here, thank you.

ALAN ANDERSON grew up cycling around London, then carried on riding around the UK and Europe, fixing his bike up himself and learning how its parts worked as he did so. Always dreaming of the 'perfect bike', he started building his own at home, and volunteers at a community bike workshop in order to develop and share his skills. This is his third book about bicycles and cycle culture.

LEE JOHN PHILLIPS is an award-winning freelance illustrator and sketchbook keeper based in Narberth, West Wales. As well as client work, he is undertaking the mammoth task of drawing every single item in his late grandfather's toolshed. To date, he has drawn over 7,400 items and sees this as his life's work. When he's not at the drawing board, Lee can be found at the coast or in the woods, carving spoons.

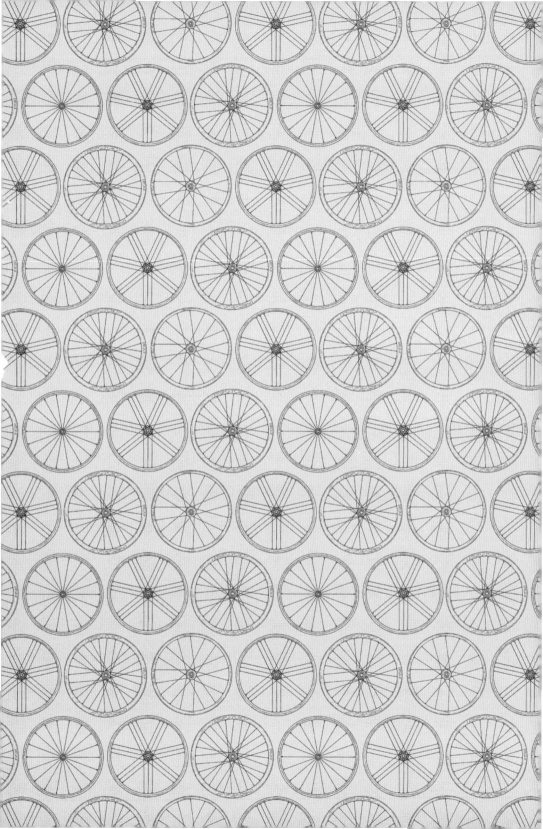